BUILDING A PROFESSION

The History of the Australian Institute of
Conveyancers (Victorian Division) and how it achieved
licensing for Conveyancers in Victoria

By
JILLEAN LUDWELL OAM

First published 2023

A self published title designed and produced by Adala Publishing
www.adalapublishing.com.au

Cover image: 'The Strongroom at the Registrar-General's Office',
from the *Illustrated Australian News*, 4 June 1877. Courtesy of the
La Trobe Picture Collection, State Library of Victoria.

A catalogue record for this
book is available from the
National Library of Australia

NATIONAL
LIBRARY
OF AUSTRALIA

ISBN 978-0-646-88700-5 (print)
ISBN 978-0-646-88701-2 (eBook)

CONVEYANCER (noun)

A person whose job is to manage the legal process of moving land or property from one owner to another.
(Cambridge Dictionary)

TABLE OF CONTENTS

GLOSSARY

Allen – Allen Consulting Group

ACCC – Australian Competition and Consumer Commission

ACT – Australian Capital Territory

ADLS – Auckland & District Law Society

AFR – Australian Financial Review

AG – Attorney-General

AGM – Annual General Meeting

AIC – Australian Institute of Conveyancers (National body)

AICVic – Australian Institute of Conveyancers (Victorian Division)

AICNSW – Australian Institute of Conveyancers (NSW Division)

AICSA – Australian Institute of Conveyancers (SA Division

AICWA – Australian Institute of Conveyancers (WA Division)

AICNT – Australian Institute of Conveyancers (NT Division)

AICTas – Australian Institute of Conveyancers (Tasmanian Division)

BLA – Business Licensing Authority

CPC – Certified Practising Conveyancer

CEO – Chief Executive Officer

CAV – Consumer Affairs Victoria

CPD – Continuing Professional Development

COAG – Council of Australian Governments

CSA – Conveyancing Society of Australia

Cth – Commonwealth

DOJ – Department of Justice

DTF – Department of Treasury and Finance

EC – Electronic Conveyancing

ECV – Electronic Conveyancing Victoria

FID – Financial Institutions Duty

Grove – Grove Conveyancing Services, Geelong

LTO – Land Titles Office

LR – Land Registry

LRC – Law Reform Commission

LPB – Legal Practice Board

LSB – Legal Services Board (formerly Legal Practice Board)

LPPA – Legal Profession Practice Act 1958

LPLC – Legal Practitioners' Liability Committee

LIJ – Law Institute Journal

LIV – Law Institute of Victoria

ILE – Institute of Legal Executives

MP – Member of Parliament

MHB – Michael Benjamin

NCC – National Competition Council

NCP – National Competition Policy

NECO – National Electronic Conveyancing Office

NSW – New South Wales

NT – Northern Territory

NZ – New Zealand

PEXA – Property Exchange Australia

Practice Act – The Practice Act 1996

Profession Act – The Profession Act 2004

PII – Professional Indemnity Insurance

QC – Queens Counsel`

Qld – Queensland

REIV – Real Estate Institute of Victoria

Registrar – Registrar of Titles

RPA – Recognised Professional Association

RIS – Regulatory Impact Statement

RMIT – Royal Melbourne Institute of Technology

RTO – Registered Training Organisation

S.32 – Section 32 of the Sale of Land Act 1962

SA – South Australia

SCAG – Standing Council of Attorneys General

SRO – State Revenue Office

TAFE – Technical and Further Education

Tas – Tasmania

Torrens – Robert Richard Torrens

TPA – Trade Practices Act 1974

TPC – Trade Practices Commission

VCA – Victorian Conveyancers' Association

VCAT – Victorian Civil and Administrative Tribunal

VETASSESS – Skills Assessment Authority

VMIA – Victorian Managed Insurance Authority

VPF – Victorian Property Fund

WA – Western Australia

PREFACE

TODAY'S BUYERS AND sellers of real estate in most States of Australia (except for Queensland and the Australian Capital Territory) take for granted that they have a choice of the type of practitioner they can employ to handle the legal paperwork involved with their conveyancing transaction – either a licensed conveyancer or a lawyer. However, this has not always been the case.

There was a brief period in the mid 1800s when 'certified conveyancers' came into existence in the young colonies of Victoria, New South Wales and Queensland via the *Attorneys Bills and Conveyancing Act 1847* (NSW) but they were eventually wiped out in the 1920s in Victoria and in the 1930s in New South Wales and Queensland and absorbed into the legal profession.

From that time all conveyancing work was undertaken by lawyers but, in many instances, the reality was that it was handled by conveyancing clerks in their employment and nominally under the lawyer's supervision. Conveyancing was regarded by lawyers as predominantly a clerical role that their clerks could handle but, in fact, that work made up a substantial part of the lawyers' income. Many of these workers were skilled at their job and enjoyed a high level of autonomy yet did not receive a salary commensurate with the importance or value of the transactions they were handling. Often they were not recognised as an important part of a law firm and a career path was not envisaged by management.

This history is predominantly about the Victorian conveyancing clerks and the remarkable story of how they opened up the market for conveyancing, competing with lawyers, and providing the public with a choice of practitioner. The path was long and challenging and was undertaken by a very determined and resilient group of professionals whose sole aim, from the end of the 1980s, was to convince the Victorian Government to regulate the conveyancing industry.

Some of the arguments made and actions taken by the legal profession in the mid 1800s against conveyancers were uncomfortably similar to those that emerged in the 1980s when conveyancers were beginning to establish their businesses. The difference between the eras is that, while certified conveyancers existed in the mid 1800s, they did not exist in large enough numbers or, research would suggest, have a sufficiently strong voice to withstand pressure from the legal profession.

Fortunately, that was not the case in the 1980s.

The campaign for licensing was carried out by a small group of conveyancers who formed the Victorian Conveyancers' Association (VCA) in 1989 (incorporating in 1991) which later became the Australian Institute of Conveyancers (Victorian Division) (AICVic) when it became the Victorian Division of the national Australian Institute of Conveyancers (AIC) in 1997.

I was one of the founding members of the Victorian Conveyancers' Association (VCA) and have held various executive positions on the Boards of the Victorian and National bodies including as Chief Executive Officer of AICVic from 2003 to 2021.

My main purpose in writing the history of the AICVic and explaining the role it played in the introduction of licensing for conveyancers, is to ensure that the younger generation of licensed conveyancers are aware of the issues that conveyancers faced and the tremendous amount of work and dedication undertaken by successive AICVic Committees and management teams (sometimes at a very great cost) which led to the introduction of the *Conveyancers Act 2006 (Vic)*.

There is still work to be done in the areas of mandating Continuing Professional Development and increasing the required experience component for licensing. The AICVic and conveyancers today have an important responsibility to ensure that standards continue to improve in order that the profession remains relevant and future generations of conveyancers are supported and encouraged to continue this worthwhile profession.

Jillean Ludwell OAM

CHAPTER 1

ORIGINS OF THE PROFESSION OF CONVEYANCER

THE ORIGINS OF the profession of conveyancers date back to medieval times in the United Kingdom where members of the profession were known as 'scriveners'. Attorneys also existed and were involved in land transactions through the 17 and 18th centuries, largely as an aspect of their work as law agents and estate managers for landholders. In the provinces, non-lawyer conveyancers competed with attorneys for work. However, in the City of London in 1712, all attorneys were prohibited from undertaking conveyancing work, as it was exclusively reserved for members of the Scriveners' Company.[1] Their influence would diminish over time as solicitors and attorneys, and even barristers, won a monopoly on the drawing of conveyances and eventually the profession of scrivener declined.

The first Australian conveyancers arrived from England to Sydney Cove in New South Wales around 1780 and were 'convict attorneys.'[2] These attorneys were not always upright honest

---

1 The Queensland Solicitors' Conveyancing Reservation: Past and Future Development – Part 1 (2009) – Mark Byrne and Reid Mortensen
2 Dale Turner's book 'Convict Attorneys' Dismembered Limbs and Certified Conveyancers 2014.' (Unpublished)

citizens and some had been convicted of perjury and forgery. They were 'stained' men and could not appear in Court.

From around 1800 to the 1820s, despite their offences, these attorneys appear to be the principal providers of property/conveyancing law in the colony. Property was an important part of the New South Wales economy and their skills were put to good use.

During the 1820s and 1830s a small class of unregulated conveyancers were drawing the deeds and parchments for citizens of the growing Colony. The part these conveyancers played in the early Colony went far beyond the service of 'professional' solicitors; they helped to create the Colony's first institutions, established legal administrations and, through the transfer of property, an expanding free economy as it evolved from military rule to a civil administration.

In time, many of the convict attorneys received a pardon and began to establish themselves as competent to undertake conveyancing and other areas of the law. There was an urgent need to secure good title to small holdings and broad acres, resulting in a demand for the services of those first conveyancers in the Colony but no-one appears to have been prosecuted for breaching the law and the business of conveyancing continued unregulated. As more land was granted by the Governor, the services of this unregulated 'profession' was in demand; the Census of 1846 directed that conveyancers were to be embraced by the Court as members of the legal profession. They mostly practised in New South Wales but some also set up practices in Melbourne, Tasmania and Brisbane.

Conveyancing was based on the British legal system (known as the old law system) which had carried over to the Colony of New South Wales and subsequently to the other Colonies of Australia. Purchasers had to trace ownership of a property via a chain of deeds, sometimes as far back as the Crown Grant (the land belonging to the Crown, i.e. the reigning sovereign of the day, and is the first freehold title to a piece of land granted by, or alienated from, the Crown). The Crown considered the land to be 'terra nullius',[1] the literal translation being 'nobody's land'. This doctrine has existed in the law of many nations throughout the development of western democracies and is based on the principle that ownership by seizure of a thing (in this case property) no-one owns, is legitimate. The Proclamation of NSW Governor Richard Bourke in 1835 implemented the legal principle of terra nullius in Australian law as the basis of British settlement. This was 47 years after the arrival of the First Fleet.

From the beginning of the Colony, Governor Philip had instructions from Britain to grant land and the first land grants went to ex-convicts. In the old law system of conveyancing each deed, i.e. transfer, mortgage etc., was accompanied by a 'memorial' which was recorded in Memorial Books. Once a property changed hands, a new deed was drawn up. It was a costly, cumbersome and time-consuming exercise. An inspection of the chain was nor-mally undertaken by solicitors' clerks who acquired a real expertise in this role.

It is clear from various newspaper articles of the time that both the legal process and people handling conveyancing, were

---

1   The doctrine of terra nullius was overturned by a decision of the High Court of Australia on 3 June 1992 in the case of Mabo v Queensland (No.2)(1992)(Mabo). The Mabo decision altered the foundation of land law in Australia and inserted the legal doctrine of native title into Australian law. The Court recognised the traditional rights of the Meriam people to their islands in the Torres Strait. The Court also held that naive title existed for all Indigenous people in Australia prior to the establishment of the British Colony of New South Wales in 1788. The decision was swiftly followed by the Native Title Act (Cth) 1992.

unsatisfactory. There was much land speculation and the system of land registration was chaotic and unreliable. In a letter to the Editor of the Victorian Portland Guardian on 15 October 1842, the writer complained that residents experienced serious inconvenience in consequence of defective titles to their landed and freehold property and endless litigation occasioned through the inaccuracies of conveyances. The article called for the testing of conveyancers in relation to their qualifications as there was evidence of low standards and incompetence. It appeared that the Supreme Court had little control over these conveyancers and the writer called for all deeds to be registered and more control to be exerted by the Supreme Court commenting might it not be proper to license conveyancers who should be responsible to some legal jurisdiction?[1]

Property conveyancing remained unregulated until 1847 when the *Attorneys' Bills and Conveyancing Act 1847 (NSW) 2 Vic 33 (Attorney Act)* was introduced which brought into existence a third branch of the legal profession. It gave the exclusive right to undertake conveyancing work to attorneys and solicitors, to barristers and to 'certificated conveyancers' who were examined and licensed by the Supreme Court to undertake land transactions and to charge for that service. It was a scheme that would be maintained in New South Wales, Victoria and Queensland into the 1930s, although the number of court-licensed conveyancers in all three colonies was so small, they did not seriously threaten the dominant market position of attorneys and solicitors.

The *NSW Attorney Act* was eventually received into Victoria via an Act called *The Application of NSW Laws to Victoria Act 14 Vic No.49.*

---

1 Portland Guardian 15 October 1842.

Early History of Conveyancing in Victoria

Melbourne was founded in 1835 at the head of Port Phillip Bay. The first land sales occurred in 1837 and the earliest Crown Grants that showed the land as alienated by the Government of New South Wales were issued from Sydney in March 1838.[1]

For the first decade of Melbourne's existence, all the memorials and records for the District of Port Phillip were held in the Sydney office of the Registrar-General of N.S.W. As home ownership escalated in Victoria, the staff could not cope with the volume of transactions, which was most unsatisfactory to the citizens of Melbourne, and in 1846 the NSW Executive Council recommended separation of Port Phillip from NSW. However, it took the British Government until 1849 to pass the legislation to separate the Port Phillip district, resulting in the Colony of Victoria coming into existence in 1851.

When the Colony of Victoria was established a new Registry was set up in Melbourne where the first land sales were recorded in the Lands Department on 7 May 1851 and Grants issued in December 1851. Land was regarded as a valuable source of wealth in the Colony.

In the same year gold was found at Clunes, near Ballarat, and 'gold fever' developed rapidly. As a result, the population of Victoria exploded over the next decade with an influx of immigrants[2], who poured into the newly proclaimed Colony seeking to make their fortune. Despite occasional slumps in 1855 and 1858, gold sparked the development of the local property market. Unlike

---

1 Safe as Houses – The History of the Victorian Land Titles Office by Robin Grow

2 Australian Property Law Journal No.24 of 2016 – article by Dr. Elena Di Marco PhD, University of Udine, Italy

NSW, these migrants were not convicts but free men, with ambition and skills who put their new found wealth into purchasing freehold property.

The media continued to report on people undertaking conveyancing for a fee who were not 'certified conveyancers' but eventually this was stopped with the introduction of the Victorian *Supreme Court Act 1890*. S.261 of the *Supreme Court Act 1890* (Vic) stated –

> '261. *Every person who shall for or in expectation of any fee gain or reward directly or indirectly draw or prepare any conveyance or other deed or instrument in writing relating to any real estate or any proceedings in law or equity (other than and except barristers or solicitors of the Supreme Court, or certificated conveyancers, and other than and except persons solely employed to engross any deed instrument or other proceeding not drawn or prepared by themselves and for their own account respectively, and other than and except public officers drawing or preparing official instruments applicable to their respective offices and in the course of their duty), shall be deemed guilty of a contempt of the Court and shall and may be punished accordingly for every such offence upon the application of any person complaining thereof, or shall for every such offence forfeit and pay the sum of Twenty pounds to be sued for and recovered in a summary way before any two or more justices of the peace and in accordance with the provisions of any Act for the time being in force relating to summary proceedings before justices of the peace.'*

With the introduction of the *Attorney Act* into Victoria, a small number of unregulated conveyancers who had been working in Victoria, applied to the Supreme Court to become 'certificated conveyancers'. There was no 'grandfathering'[1] arrangement, so conveyancers had to sit exams set by the Master of Equity of the Supreme Court, however the Act did provide legitimacy for conveyancers who had passed the exam and removed those unable to pass the exam.

The Law List of the Supreme Court of 1863 discloses the names of those first certificated conveyancers –

Brahe, William Alexander	*– Date of Certificate –*	*1856*
Dry, Richard	*– " " –*	*No date*
Forwood, Charles Rossiter	*– " " –*	*1853*
Garlick, William Shuckburgh	*– " " –*	*1854*
Hewitt, Arthur	*– " " –*	*1856*
Johnson, Henry	*– " " –*	*1853*
McGreevy, John	*– " " –*	*1859*
Snowden, Arthur	*– " " –*	*1862*
Trollope, William Thomas	*– " " –*	*1853*

In the late 1850s land speculation was rife, with large profits to be made. The old law system of deeds was too expensive and complicated and not fit for purpose, so the Victorian Government began seeking a better method of handling the transfer of property. The Geelong Advertiser and Squatters Advocate of 23 March 1847 contained an article by Mr. James Stewart, an eminent writer on conveyancing, speaking to landowners on the advantages and necessity of a free trade in land –

---

1 'Grandfathering' means that a person operating in a pre-existing occupation can continue to operate, despite a later rule for new entrants to the occupation being introduced, i.e. they are exempt from having to comply with the new rules.

'If you can buy land more easily' he says 'or sell land more easily, or borrow money more easily on your land, this is a direct benefit to you... The endeavours should now be to obtain –

1. *Simplicity and uniformity of tenure*
2. *Easy, cheap and expeditious modes of transfer*
3. *Shorter and more simpler deeds*
4. *A greater certainty as to time completing the sale and mortgage of land*
5. *Some mode of shortening enquiry as to title.*

These desirable objects would be materially aided by a general official map of the country and a general register of titles.'[1]

Neither New South Wales nor Tasmania could offer a solution to the need for a simpler system, as their dealings were based on the same deeds-based system. The Government therefore turned to South Australia which had introduced a more simplified system, known as the Torrens system.

Introduction of the Torrens System

Robert Richard Torrens was a Protestant Irish immigrant, born in Cork in 1814 and educated at Trinity College, Dublin, Ireland. He worked in the Port of London before marrying and emigrating to South Australia in 1841 where he became a Collector of Customs.

His father was Colonel Robert Torrens, Chairman of the Colonisation Commission for South Australia. Torrens was not a trained lawyer, but he had a desire to reform the method of transferring property which brought him into conflict with the South Australian legal profession. He was a man of passion and

---

1 Geelong Advertiser and Squatters Advocate 23 March 1847

some arrogance who was elected to the South Australian House of Assembly in 1857.[1]

He formed a friendship with Dr Ulrich Hubbe, a lawyer of German heritage, who had written articles published in the SA papers calling for conveyancing reform. Dr Hubbe was influential in the formation of the Torrens system.

The Torrens system simplified the whole confused process of land transfer by reducing the number of deeds involved into one document.[2] This document, which was entered into the official Government Register at the Land Titles Office, became the sole valid claim to ownership of property and allowed a person to show that they not only owned the land, but also showed the area and measurements of that land. The system removed the need to establish whether there was a good 'root of title' by scrutinising all the documents that made up the chain of title from the original Government Grant of an estate. Transferring land became a simple, straightforward process and made ownership conclusive and indefeasible (that which cannot be made void or forfeited).

Indefeasibility[3] is a central element of the Torrens legislation and has been since the original Act. It was considered reasonable that the State, through the Registrar, should guarantee the proprietor's title. After all, it was the Registrar that created the proprietor's title by an act of registration. If a mistake was made in registering the proprietor's interest, or should a person have become the proprietor through fraud of another, the Registrar, and through the Registrar, the State, should stand behind that registration. It was therefore no longer necessary to reach beyond

---

1 The Torrens System – R.T.J. Stein & M.A. Stone 1991 – Butterworths
2 Land Rights for Everyone – State Library of South Australia Archive.
3 'Safe as Houses – the History of the Victorian Land Titles Office' by Robin Grow – p.60

the Government record to trace back any chain of deeds of previous transactions to show the land was validly owned.

To back up this guarantee, provision was also made for an 'assurance fund' to be established to enable anyone who might have been unfairly or accidentally disposed of their land to receive compensation.[1]

Another fundamental principle of the system is that the title to the land, and to interests in land, depends on registration at the Land Titles Office. Once a Transfer of Land is lodged and registered at the Land Titles Office, a duplicate title is issued back to the proprietor, either the owner or a mortgagee.

The system was well suited to the rapidly expanding colony and provided benefits to the individual, government and society alike. It was simple, reliable, prompt and affordable, offering an unprecedented level of title security, giving landowners greater piece of mind and improved access to credit.[2]

The South Australian newspapers of the day advocated for the reform of the conveyancing process and despite being vehemently opposed by the legal profession, who could see their generous fees diminishing, the *Real Property Act 1858* (SA) came into operation. In fact, when the Torrens system was first introduced by the South Australian Parliament in the 1880s, some solicitors placed a black ban on handling land transfers where the Torrens system was used. The Government retaliated by amending the original Act in 1860 to allow for the introduction of a strike-breaking force of 'land brokers' to transfer titles under this new system. These land

1 The Birth of Land Brokers 1987 – Extract from 'Lawmakers and Wayward Whigs – Government and Law in South Australia 1836–1986' by Alex Castles and Michael Harris.
2 Torrens in the 21st Century by Simon Libbis, Register General of South Australia, and Matthew Carroll, Project Officer, Office of the Registrar General – 2008

brokers were laymen, not lawyers, who took over the conveyancing process in South Australia and they retain it to this day. They are now known as 'registered conveyancers'. The appointment of land brokers in South Australia was instrumental in ensuring that the administration of the Torrens system did not break down in its early stages. No other jurisdiction in Australia that introduced the Torrens system created land brokers.

In 1858, Torrens gave up his seat in the Legislative Assembly of the South Australian Parliament to take up the position of Registrar-General to undertake the task of organising the department appointed to administer the *Real Property Act*.[1] His real reason for accepting the appointment was that he believed that unless he organised the implementation of the new system, it would fail. This belief had arisen from the many obstacles which had been placed in his way during the campaign for reform, spearheaded by the legal profession and the judiciary.

He returned to England in 1863 and was knighted in 1872. *'He received his knighthood because of his colonial services in general but, in particular, for his introduction of the Real Property Act.'*[2]

The Torrens System is introduced into Victoria

By the early 1860s it was clear that the South Australian Torrens system was a great success resulting in much interest in Victoria.

An important, wealthy Victorian businessman (and actor), George Coppin, who had spent time in South Australia and befriended Torrens, played a key role in the introduction of the Torrens land reform legislation into the Victorian Parliament.

---

1 The Torrens System – Title by Registration: its History and Nomenclature – by R.T.J. Stein and M.A. Stone – Butterworths 1991.
2 Torrens of the Torrens System by G. Jessup – unpublished – State Library of South Australia (Archives) Adelaide 1950 at 9.27.

Coppin introduced the *Real Property Bill* into the Victorian Parliament on 30 November 1859, which was a carbon copy of the South Australian legislation. Robert Torrens visited Melbourne in 1860 for a lecture tour to promote the reform.

By March 1862, virtually every newspaper in the colony of Victoria was calling for its immediate introduction. There were even petitions organised; 4000 people signed a petition in Geelong and another 6000 signed in Melbourne.[1]

In 1862 the existing certified conveyancers of the Supreme Court moved a petition in the Parliament praying that, if the *Real Property Bill* were passed, they might be admitted to practise as attorneys. This petition was presented by Mr. Coppin, who moved the second reading of the *Real Property Bill*[2] and, in a speech of some length, explained and defended it.

It was a controversial reform which was bitterly opposed by the Victorian Attorney-General, Richard Ireland, and much of the legal profession. It took some time to pass the Victorian Parliament and it was only after intense lobbying by both the press and the public that the *Real Property Bill* was passed.

The legislation finally passed through Parliament in May 1862. Only the Royal Assent was now necessary to make it law but the Attorney-General, Richard Ireland, said he would advise the Governor to refuse the sanction of the Crown to the *Bill*. Parliamentarians threatened that, if he did, they would block supply and force an election on the issue of the Torrens system. Cabinet was divided on the question, but ultimately the Governor chose to provide assent and the legislation came into force on

---

1 Melbourne Herald 5 March 1862.
2 Melbourne Herald 9 April 1862

2 October 1862[1] and the system subsequently spread throughout Australia. Queensland was the first colony to adopt the Torrens system in 1861, followed by Tasmania, Victoria and New South Wales in 1862 and Western Australia in 1874. Over time, many overseas countries went on to adopt the Torrens system, including New Zealand and British Columbia in Canada.

To quote Dr Greg Taylor from *'Safe as Houses – the History of the Victorian Land Titles Office by Robin Grow'* –

> *'It is an appalling reflection on the legal profession in both South Australia and Victoria that, with a few honourable exceptions, what may without exaggeration be described as one of the greatest reforms of the law of property in the history of the common-law world ..... occurred not only without the help of most of the experts in the field concerned, but **despite** some of them.'*

Whilst the Torrens system was to become the primary method of land registration in Victoria, the deeds system (referred to as the old law system) remained in operation. The 1862 *Real Property Act* provided for an ability to bring old law land under the Torrens system but it was an involved and time-consuming business requiring specialist skills. The Victorian Land Registry has attempted to facilitate conversion of all land from old law to Torrens title over the years, but today there are still small pockets of land yet to be converted.

In August 1866 the *Transfer of Land Act* (Vic) came into force and the position of Registrar of Titles was created and an Office of Titles opened in William Street, Melbourne. However, by the 1870s the office had outgrown the site due to Melbourne's

---

1 Safe as Houses – The History of the Victorian Land Titles Office by Robin Grow – p.14

property boom and a new office was built in 1877 on the corner of Queen and Lt. Lonsdale Streets, Melbourne.

Today the task of searching titles and instruments is undertaken electronically.

CHAPTER 2

REVIEWS, ENQUIRIES AND CHANGES
IN THE 1980S

DESPITE THE INTRODUCTION of the Torrens system into Victoria, unlike South Australia, land brokers were not established and conveyancing was handled by solicitors and a small band of certified conveyancers. However, these Court-licensed conveyancers were marked for extinction with the passing of the *Legal Profession Practice Act 1915* (Vic) prohibiting anyone other than a barrister or solicitor from preparing a conveyance for a fee. Instead, these conveyancers were given the option of seeking admission to the Supreme Court as solicitors. Over time, the independent occupation of conveyancer died out and the work remained in the hands of the legal profession until the early 1980s.

In the late 1970s there had been multiple media articles in Victoria calling for an overhaul of conveyancing law and, in particular, calling for the Victorian Government to review the high fees being charged by solicitors in this area of the law. Solicitors had traditionally used a method of charging for their service known as the 'ad valorem' method. Ad valorem, meaning 'according to the value' meant charging a percentage of the value of the land, rather than a fixed amount.

The Victorian Government finally commissioned a *Committee of Inquiry into Conveyancing* (known as the Dawson Enquiry). The

Final Report was handed down on 19 August 1980. The two main recommendations were –

- To amend the *Estate Agents Act 1980* (Vic) to provide that an estate agent who filled up or obtained a signature to any contract of sale prepared by any solicitor or barrister or any standard form contract approved by the Law Institute of Victoria or prescribed by rules under the Act, shall not be guilty of an offence against S.93 of the *Legal Profession Practice Act 1958* (Vic). This section prohibited an 'unqualified' person from drawing, filling up or preparing any instrument creating or regulating rights between parties or relating to real or personal property where the act is done for or in expectation of any fee, gain or reward.
- To introduce a 'cooling off' period of 3 days in which a purchaser could withdraw from any contract that they had entered into, in many instances following persuasive sales techniques from the estate agents. There had been provision in South Australia for a cooling off period since 1974 and in New South Wales since 1978. Naturally the Real Estate and Stock Institute of Victoria (as the Real Estate Institute of Victoria was known then) argued against the introduction of a cooling off period, believing such a move would complicate negotiating a sale and delay closure of a contract.

The Dawson Committee believed that the *caveat emptor (let the buyer beware)* approach in Victoria had its shortcomings and considered that the principle should be reversed, at least to a limited extent, so that it became *caveat vendor*. Although the Law Institute of Victoria supported this change, it had reservations about the amount of information which the vendor should be required to supply. The Real Estate and Stock Institute of Victoria supported the *caveat vendor* principle if it led to the early signing of a binding contract of sale, but believed that the disclosure of information should be restricted to information relating to title and that the vendor should not be required to produce relevant property certificates before a contract was concluded. No doubt their opinion was based on the time it might take to obtain those relevant certificates and the delay this may cause in getting a contract signed.

It was apparent to the Committee that the Victorian Titles Office was inadequately housed, equipped and staffed, and there was an urgent need for the introduction of modern techniques in the recording of information, in maintaining records, keeping them up to date and in registering dealings with land. The system needed to be updated from a manual system to modern technology; a computerised Register needed to be created; a reference map structure needed to be created and each parcel, and each record relating to each parcel, needed to be identified by unique parcel identifiers. It was anticipated that this modernisation process would take ten years to complete.[1]

The Committee also commented that the State of Victoria was rapidly falling behind New South Wales and South Australia which had already commenced programmes for the full conversion of their land registries to introduce modern techniques.

A presentation given at the Eastern Solicitors' Association of Victoria's Annual Conference on 14 November 1981 by the Hon. Mr. Justice Michael Kirby, Chairman of the Australian Law Reform Commission at that time, highlighted some worrying predictions for the legal profession, if computerisation of land titles and creation of a land use database went ahead. He feared it would perform a great deal of the routine work currently done by

---

1 Committee of Inquiry into Conveyancing – Further and Final Report
   – Daryl Dawson QC (Chairman), David A. Crawford, James W. Davies –
   1980.

solicitors in the land conveyancing business. '*The effects will be, in part, for the good but they will also pose problems*', he predicted.

Although his presentation, '*The Future of Legal Practice or Does it Have One?*', attracted some criticism from the legal profession, he was concerned that lawyers should recognise what was coming and start planning for greater diversification.

He went on to say –

> '*the prospect of computerisation of land conveyancing is a very serious one in a profession which depends as to 50% of its work upon the work of land conveyancing... Despite the Dawson Report in Victoria, it seems likely to me that lawyers will, in those States where the monopoly in paid legal conveyancing persists, lose that monopoly protection and have to compete, as they do in Western Australia and South Australia, with land agents. ...In short, the lawyers' involvement in land conveyancing may change somewhat. It will not evaporate entirely.*'

We now have a fully electronic system for undertaking settlements which is mandatory in the States of Victoria, New South Wales, South Australia and Western Australia. There are also strong and dedicated conveyancing professions in those States, competing very efficiently with lawyers.

Changes to the Sale of Land Act 1962 (Vic)

It took some time for the Victorian Government to implement the recommendations of the Dawson Committee, but in 1983 the Victorian Government introduced a vendor's statement pursuant to S.32 of the *Sale of Land Act 1962* (Vic). This new disclosure statement, provided by the vendor to the purchaser, set out details of planning, rates, building permits etc. and included a copy of the title and plan of the land being sold. The vendor's statement was mandatory (i.e. it could not be contracted out of), and had to be provided to the purchaser before they could enter into a contract of sale to purchase a property.

At the same time a cooling off provision was also introduced for residential property to provide a purchaser of land with some protection against impetuous buying or persuasive techniques used by some estate agents. The three business day cooling off period started from the day the purchaser signed the contract.

The vendor's statement was quickly accepted by the consumer, as it gave a buyer some comfort with regard to what land they were purchasing and the restrictions associated with that land. The process involved employing a solicitor to prepare a vendor's statement, attaching a copy of the title search and plan of the land together with copies of property certificates. This would be sent to the selling agent who, once they had found a buyer, would provide them with a copy of the vendor's statement and fill out a 'sale note' which was a brief document detailing the parties, the price and the basic terms of the sale, but subject always to a solicitor preparing a formal contract of sale.

The *Estate Agents Act 1980* (Vic) was also amended so that the sale note was reinvented as a contract note, allowing the real estate agent to 'fill up' this document, which then resulted in a binding contract. The relevant amendment to the *Estate Agents Act 1980* (Vic) meant that by 'filling up' the contract note, real estate agents would not be accused of holding themselves out to be a 'solicitor' and accordingly did not fall foul of the law.

This step brought about a significant change to the industry. Once the real estate agent was able to complete a binding contract between the vendor and purchaser, there was no longer a necessity for a solicitor to prepare a more formal contract of sale (although they were still able to prepare formal contracts).

Clerks seek a better career path

For many years legal firms had employed clerks in their offices to handle the more practical side of a solicitor's work. These clerks became quite specialised in a range of areas of the law, such as conveyancing, probate, litigation, etc. The majority were women who had left school at 15 or 16 with typing and shorthand skills and went on to become efficient secretaries. Some more enlightened solicitors paid for their clerks to be trained by undertaking specialised courses being taught at the Royal Melbourne Institute of Technology (RMIT) and other colleges, but most law firms did not provide training or advancement, preferring their clerks to remain in the background with little acknowledgement of their contribution to the firm's income.

Many conveyancing clerks felt that their career prospects were limited within solicitors' offices, despite running substantial departments and having a large degree of autonomy. However, under the *Legal Profession Practice Act 1958* (Vic), they were unable to become a partner in a legal firm or share in the profits, despite being responsible for a substantial slice of their firm's income. This was before compulsory superannuation, so there was no incentive for the clerks to remain with a law firm if they had the ambition to open up a business.

There was a general acceptance at the time amongst the conveyancing industry that there were two main barriers to conveyancers becoming self-employed – the preparation of a formal contract of sale binding the parties and the preparation of a transfer of land – the document that would ultimately be lodged for registration at the Titles Office to transfer the property from the vendor to the purchaser. Once real estate agents were able to complete a binding contract note, that only left the transfer of land as the contentious document. In reality, the vendor's statement was not a binding legal document, but merely a stand-alone statement, preparatory to entering into a contract of sale.

In the 1980s some brave conveyancers decided to go it alone and set themselves up in business. They were able to arrange for the transfer of land to be approved by a solicitor (for a fee) and with the contract note being prepared by a real estate agent, they were able to prepare the vendor's statement and carry out the remaining work involved in the transaction.

These conveyancing businesses began to flourish and were popular with the consumer and the real estate industry, undertaking the process for a vastly reduced fee. Many conveyancers had significant experience, having worked for many years in legal offices, had completed legal courses at Technical and Further Education (TAFE) colleges and others had achieved the status of Fellows of the Institute of Legal Executives (ILE), an organisation providing training for para-legals. Seeing no career path within a legal office, they accepted the challenge of going out on their own and becoming self-employed.

CHAPTER 3

THE BEGINNINGS OF THE VICTORIAN PROFESSION

THE ESTABLISHMENT OF a conveyancing business was not without risk. These companies were beginning to gain traction with the consumer and were impacting the solicitors' monopoly. Solicitors were particularly frustrated that the consumers made little distinction between the services offered by solicitors and those offered by conveyancers, and often just chose the cheapest price without understanding the intricacies of a conveyancing transaction. In addition, some of their own colleagues were 'colluding' with conveyancers to get around the prohibition of them preparing legal documents and breaching the *Legal Profession Practice Act 1958* (Vic). Some solicitors were prepared to make an arrangement to carry out the 'legal work' component of a conveyancing transaction and accept a fee from a conveyancer in order that the conveyancer could operate their own business.

Bearing in mind that the Law Institute of Victoria (LIV) had a regulatory role under the *Legal Profession Practice Act 1958* (Vic), it was constantly alert to any 'unqualified' people offering conveyancing services. The LIV argued that these people were *'holding themselves out to be a solicitor'* and it prosecuted them for breaches of the *Legal Profession Practice Act 1958* (Vic). Several conveyancers found themselves in Court defending their activities, arguing that they were not preparing legal documents – the contract of sale was prepared/filled up by real estate agents, and the conveyancers retained a solicitor to approve the transfer of land.

Despite the LIV declaring that conveyancers were 'unqualified', and that a person required a law degree to undertake conveyancing, it was evident that the role did not require a degree. Conveyancers undertook the more practical work involved in a conveyancing transaction and they also required some knowledge of property law. In fact, RMIT, (one of the most respected tertiary colleges in Australia) and a number of other Registered Training Organisations (RTOs) had, for a number of years, been running quasi-legal courses. The Associate Diploma of Business (Legal Practice), which was offered by RMIT, was previously known as the Articled Clerks' Course, enabling a graduate to meet the educational requirements to become a solicitor. A number of well-respected people gained their practising certificates after completing that course, notably in 1983 Rob Hulls, Attorney-General in the Bracks/Brumby Labor Government.

In an article in The Australian Financial Review on 25 September 1991, Michael Stutchbury commented –

'Conveyancing is ideally suited to being performed by certified paralegals who have passed a couple of years of well-focussed education. The long-standing SA example suggests that service quality, customer satisfaction and consumer protection against fraud can be maintained.'

Despite knowing there were people running conveyancing businesses who had minimal educational qualifications in property law, or who had even been struck off the Supreme Court roll, consumers, looking to pay a lower price for their conveyancing transaction, were not deterred.

By the end of the 1980s, there were a number of highly experienced, educated and professional conveyancers running their businesses who believed that a licensing scheme was necessary to provide the legitimacy that the operators desired. It is difficult to know how many conveyancing businesses were operating at this time, because few of them advertised, for fear of being investigated and perhaps prosecuted by the LIV. They relied instead on word-of-mouth referrals.

In 1991 the LIV sent many conveyancers a letter[1] asking for the name of the solicitor who undertook the 'legal work' on their behalf and threatening prosecution if they were seen to be breaching the *Legal Profession Practice Act*.

The letter galvanised a handful of conveyancers into action; the members of the group that held that first meeting were Trevor Cousley (the first President), Maree Cousley, Mary Cocking, Ellen Norton, Pauline Barrow and the writer. The contents of the letter from the LIV were analysed and discussion took place on what response should be given and how to map out a way forward for the profession. That path was to form the Victorian Conveyancers' Association (VCA) on 29 April 1991 (later to become the Australian Institute of Conveyancers (Victorian Division) (AICVic) when it became the Victorian Division of the Australian Institute of Conveyancers (AIC) in 1997).

These dedicated conveyancers, well experienced in their vocation and passionate about their right to be on an equal footing with lawyers, were already running successful businesses which were built on providing expertise and empathy to their clients.

---

1   Letter to Conveyancers from Law Institute of Victoria 1991

They met fortnightly with the aim of developing a plan to gain more members to become stronger, and to design a strategy to convince the Victorian Government to regulate conveyancers.

The VCA quickly established itself as a strong, vocal body and, from its inception, introduced benchmarks and standards for its members (designed to give the consumer confidence when employing their services to act in a conveyancing transaction). They immediately established a Code of Conduct and required every member to take out a professional indemnity insurance policy to cover them for negligence. These steps were necessary to counteract actions by lawyers attempting to undermine confidence in conveyancing businesses as they feared the loss of lucrative conveyancing income.

To ensure that members could comply with the legislation surrounding who could undertake 'legal work', VCA arranged for a solicitor to be available to all members for a fee. It was not easy to find a solicitor, but on 1 July 1996 Michael Benjamin became the VCA retained solicitor. Michael had been a member of the Police Force since 1978 and later completed a law degree at Monash University. In 1993 he opened Dingley Conveyancing Services and became a member of the VCA. Michael was a crucial part of the Association's development, assisting members to comply with the *Legal Practice Act 1996* (Vic) and providing a 'hotline' service for legal problems that members may experience.

Another important task for the VCA was to establish a dedicated conveyancing course and an approach was made to RMIT which had been running the *Associate Diploma of Business (Legal Practice)* for some years. This was a broad legal course covering many areas of the law and designed to educate paralegals within legal offices. Eventually a course was developed which contained relevant conveyancing subjects including business subjects and areas of the law which could affect a conveyancing transaction, such as company law, probate, etc. By the end of 1994 the *Diploma of Conveyancing* was approved and began in mid-1996.

Whilst professional indemnity insurance was compulsory for practising solicitors, there was no such requirement for conveyancers and many non-VCA member conveyancers did not hold it. A solicitor's policy did not cover his/her work undertaken for conveyancers and some took out separate professional indemnity insurance to cover this role.

Reviews and Actions

In 1992 the Commonwealth Parliament passed the *Mutual Recognition Act* (Cth), the principal aim of which was to remove artificial barriers to interstate trade and goods caused by regulatory differences across Australian States and Territories and to improve the mobility of labour. S.17 of the Act stated that a person who is registered in one State as an 'occupation' was entitled to be registered in a second State for the equivalent occupation. This worked for some trades, such as electricians or plumbers, but because of the differences in the scope of work undertaken by conveyancers in the States and Territories where conveyancers were regulated (let alone where they were not regulated), it was disputed whether the equivalence of occupation between States and Territories existed.

In the same year, the Council of Australian Governments (COAG) set up a Committee of Enquiry chaired by Professor Fred Hilmer to look at ways to generate more competition in Australia. The report of that Committee found that many restrictions on competition were because of government regulation and the use of the *Trade Practices Act 1974* (Cth) would not remove those restrictions.

COAG agreed to review anti-competitive legislation to ensure that legislation did not restrict competition unless it could be demonstrated that –
- The benefits of the restriction on the community as a whole outweighed the costs.
- The objectives of the legislation could only be achieved by restricting competition.

Following the recommendations of the Hilmer Committee report, the Commonwealth, State and Territory Governments agreed to develop a National Competition Policy (NCP) under the auspices of the Trade Practices Commission (TPC). Part of the competition policy was to look at Part IV of the *Trade Practices Act 1974* (Cth) from which some public enterprises and professionals were protected from market forces. This would have important implications for the legal profession, particularly in relation to its conveyancing monopoly in Victoria.

The Chair of the TPC, Professor Allan Fels, released a discussion paper entitled *'The Legal Profession, Conveyancing and the Trade Practices Act'*. Amongst other options, the paper sought comment on a proposal *'that non-lawyers be permitted to supply conveyancing services for a fee'*. The TPC paper also acknowledged that South Australia, Western Australia and Northern Territory allowed conveyancers to perform property conveyancing and that the New South Wales Government had recently announced that it would legislate to permit non-lawyer conveyancers to operate under specified conditions.

It considered two options for regulating those who could perform services for a fee, namely –
- Certification – which would set certain minimum standards and provide information to consumers about competence of service providers without restricting entry into the market.

- Licensing – which restricts entry by prescribing minimum qualifying standards on education, experience, character and conduct and insists on mandatory insurance cover.

In its submission to the TPC, the VCA outlined the current unsatisfactory position in Victoria for conveyancers and the fact that conveyancing businesses were operating in a grey area and called for certification or licensing of conveyancers to ensure that those who were operating met a reasonable standard of education and experience and could undertake the legal work component of a transaction. Members of the VCA were required to hold professional indemnity insurance but some operators did not, leaving the consumer in a precarious situation if negligence occurred. In addition, fidelity insurance (*see below) was not available to conveyancers which would compensate a consumer if a conveyancer stole their money.

The basic principle of establishing such a fund is to protect the public against loss and to engender confidence in the system.

In August 1993 the Hilmer report recommended a national strategy for the implementation of 'competition principles' that had been agreed to by Australian heads of government.

---

* A fidelity fund exists to protect the public against loss as a result of misuse or misappropriation of trust money or property by a conveyancer, a lawyer or a real estate agent or other professional. The fund is compulsory and is contributed to by the lawyer/conveyancer/estate agent so that if misuse or misappropriation of trust monies or property occurs, the fund compensates the victim. In the case of lawyers, a fidelity fund has been in place for many years and is administered by the Legal Practitioners Liability Committee (LPLC). In the case of conveyancers and estate agents, the Victorian Property Fund (VPF) has been established under the *Estate Agents Act 1980* (Vic) and is administered by Consumer Affairs Victoria (CAV). Income to the VPF comes mainly from –

- Licence fees paid by estate agents and conveyancers
- Interest on estate agents' and conveyancers' trust accounts

In due course the Federal Government passed the *Competition Policy Reform Act* (Cth) amending the *Trade Practices Act 1974* (Cth). The amendments to Part IV took effect in August 1995. The National Competition Council (NCC) came into existence to handle policy and advisory functions and the TPC became the Australian Competition and Consumer Commission (ACCC).

This meant that professional partnerships, such as lawyers, would now come under National Competition Policy (NCP) which was designed to encourage the States and Territories to enact their own competition legislation by July 1996.

During this time there were two other important reviews under way. One was by the Law Reform Commission of Victoria which considered the need for the present limits on restrictive trade practices legislation in the context of the wider debate about competition and micro economic reform. It noted that most legal practitioners, like other professional service providers, were not subject to any pro-competition rules and on 6 May 1992, it tabled its report to Parliament recommending that the Commonwealth *Trade Practices Act 1974* apply to the legal profession; it said –

> '*the only way to prevent lawyers maintaining anti-competitive ethical rules is to subject them to the scrutiny of the Trade Practices Commission.*'[1]

The other review was established by the Federal Attorney-General, Michael Lavarch in October 1993 – the Access to Justice Advisory Committee – to consider ways in which the Commonwealth justice and legal system could be reformed to enhance access to justice and make the legal system fairer. The Chairman was Ronald Sackville, QC. Other Committee

---

1 Law Reform Commission of Victoria – Access to the law: Restrictions on legal practice Report No.47, 1992 para 52.

Members were Marcia Neave (who had been a Professor of Law at Monash University and also a Law Reform Commissioner for Victoria and NSW) and Colin Neave (who practised as a Solicitor in the private sector until 1987, and had been Chief Executive of three public sector organisations). Both Marcia and Colin Neave went on to play an important part in this history in the early 2000s.

The Committee released its report on 2 May 1994 and its Overview said that –

> 'In developing an Action Plan …. The Committee has taken account of a number of principles, including competition principles, that should apply to the legal services market, thereby bringing about a more flexible and efficient legal profession.'

In considering the regulation of the legal profession, the report noted that –

> 'If the exclusive right of lawyers to perform legal services is framed too broadly, consumers are likely to be denied the chance to purchase services from providers (such as conveyancers) who may be prepared to provide them at lower prices than lawyers.'

The report then recommended a number of Actions –

Action 3.1 the *Trade Practices Act 1974* (Cth) should be applied to the legal profession in Australia as part of a coordinated national strategy for the application of the Act to all businesses and professions.

Action 3.2 – Governments of all States should vest the regulatory functions relating to the legal profession in a statutory body, independent of professional associations.

At page 108, para 3.117 the report stated –

> 'We acknowledge that the public interest in maintaining high standards of legal service provision needs to be protected.

However, we know of no evidence that the work currently being performed by paralegals is inadequate or poses a significant threat to consumers. The Trade Practices Commission's assessment of conveyancing in those jurisdictions where it has been exposed to non-lawyer competition indicated that prices had been reduced without reduction in service quality.'

Action 3.3 – There is merit in further pursuing the removal of the legislated reservation of legal work to lawyers and allowing people with appropriate skills and training to undertake legal work in specified areas of law.

Action 3.4 The requirements for entry to the legal services market should be examined by the proposed National Advisory Council on legal services to determine the standards of entry that would maximise competition in the legal services market but protect the public interest by ensuring competence among those permitted to provide legal services to clients.[1]

The TPC released its preliminary report in November 1992 calling for conveyancing laws to be freed up nationally. Non-lawyers should be able to supply conveyancing services for a fee, reducing costs to the consumer –

Jurisdictions which are still limiting conveyancing to lawyers appear to be restricting competition unnecessarily' ...

the report said. It also suggested that

'Certification, rather than licensing of conveyancing suppliers, would set minimum standards and provide information to

---

1 Report of Access to Justice Advisory Committee – Action Plan – 1994.

consumers about the competence of service providers without restricting entry into the market.[1]

There was also strong support from the press and in its editorial of 17 November 1992, The Age newspaper commented –

'Even the word "conveyancing" sounds archaic and arcane, suggesting a guild of highly priced professionals. Lawyers in Victoria, Queensland and Tasmania are anxious to retain their lucrative monopoly rights to transfer property title for a fee. The Trade Practices Commission is eager to open the conveyancing business to non-lawyers, arguing that the public would benefit from greater competition and lower costs. The Trade Practices Commission argues a cogent case, based on economic principles and on the experience of States where solicitors have lost their exclusive rights over conveyancing. However, it cannot itself bring about the reforms it advocates, but has to encourage the public to accept its reasoning and, more particularly, persuade politicians to amend the present restrictive laws....

In Victoria, the lifting of fee advertising bans and the availability of do-it-yourself conveyancing kits has encouraged some price competition among solicitors, but fees are mostly still significantly higher than in States where the legal monopoly has been abolished......

Solicitors should be free to continue to offer conveyancing services but, like the Trade Practices Commission, we see no reason for this privilege to be restricted to the legal profession. We agree with the Trade Practices Commission that overseas and interstate experience suggests that the public would benefit from access to other suitably qualified providers without incurring unacceptable risks.

1 Trade Practices Commission – Preliminary Report November 1992.

Such conveyancers would develop a specialised expertise adequate for all but the most complicated transfers. The Trade Practices Commission favours a certification system rather than restrictive licensing for conveyancers to ensure minimum standards and competence, although the public might be better protected by mandatory insurance cover. The Trade Practices Commission initiative will test the Kennett Government's dedication to its professed commitment to deregulation, competition and consumer choice.'[1]

In its final report in 1994 on the legal profession, the TPC found that it was *heavily over-regulated and in urgent need of comprehensive reform.* It was concerned that structural regulations made it difficult for new players (including non-lawyers) to move into the market. It also said that the *Trade Practices Act* 1974 (Cth) should apply in full to lawyers.[2]

Unsurprisingly, the LIV strongly rejected the TPC's findings. Its then President, Dr Gordon Hughes, stated that Victoria already had healthy competition and that with liberal advertising rules and the availability of simple information already in existence, consumers were well informed and shopped around for the best price and service. He went on to say –

'For that reason we are not particularly concerned by the report …. Conveyancing companies could already operate in Victoria, provided legal services were done by qualified lawyers.'[3]

In November 1992, the Real Estate Institute of Victoria (REIV) sent a notice to its members warning them against recommending to their clients that they use a conveyancing company because of the lack of protection of trust monies, stating –

1 The Age Editorial – 17 November 1992.
2 Trade Practices Commission Final Report – 1994.
3 Comments by Dr Gordon Hughes – Law Institute Journal October 1992.

'Clearly the safest course of action is to recommend that clients use a solicitor for all their conveyancing requirements.'[1]

The VCA sent a swift response objecting to these instructions and reminding them of the professionalism of many conveyancers, in particular, VCA members.

The LIV and its members also ran a vocal campaign targetting consumers, recommending that they not use the services of a conveyancer as they could misuse monies held in their trust accounts and were not regulated, unlike members of the LIV.

To counteract this campaign, VCA recommended to its members not to open a trust account, arguing that if a client was required to provide funds for a settlement, they could provide those funds to the conveyancer via a bank cheque payable to the third party connected to their settlement. Another factor at the time was that Financial Institutions Duty (FID) was applicable, a duty levied by all Australian States and Territories (except Queensland) on deposits going into bank accounts. Using third party bank cheques meant that no FID was applicable. (The duty was abolished on 1 July 2001.)

At the Annual General Meeting (AGM) of the Property Law Section of the LIV on 4 November 1992, the Chairman, Frank Lynch, said –

'One unfortunate aspect of the present economic climate has been the jump in negligence claims against a number of solicitors involved in property transactions which will impact in the form of an increase in our professional indemnity insurance premiums…. The intrusion of non-lawyers into the area of conveyancing is a concern for both the profession and the community.'[2]

---

1 Letter to Members from REIV – November 1992.
2 LIV Property Law Bulletin – December 1992.

The Solicitors Guarantee Fund was the lawyers' fidelity fund and had been established for many years under the control of the LIV. It was predominantly made up of interest earned on solicitors' trust accounts and had grown to a sizeable sum. However, there had been a number of claims including a substantial claim against the Fund by the clients of Stanley Myer Rosenberg who sued LIV for $25,000,000. Rosenberg[1] was first suspected of serious fraud in 1989 but instead of calling in the Police, the LIV investigated him internally. It took six years to bring him to trial and he was finally found guilty and sentenced to five years' gaol for defrauding his clients.

Also at the LIV's AGM on 4 November 1992, discussion took place between members in relation to the licensing of conveyancers and the majority voted overwhelmingly to send a message to the Council that they did not endorse the LIV taking any initiative to bring about licensing of conveyancers.

The pressure was mounting for conveyancers to take a more unified approach to lobbying the Victorian Government to introduce regulation which would provide legitimacy and recognition needed to counteract the actions of the legal profession.

---

1 Aust. Financial Review article by Richard Salmon 9 May 1995

CHAPTER 4

CONVEYANCERS' TASKFORCE

WITH THE EMERGENCE of conveyancing businesses during the 1980s came divergent views about how conveyancers should be regulated. The VCA was only one of a number of voices calling for the Victorian Government to introduce a licensing regime for conveyancers.

'Do-it-Yourself' kits had emerged in the late 1970s and started to gain traction, marketed to the consumer as a means of undertaking their own conveyancing paperwork, eliminating the need to employ a lawyer and pay lawyers' fees. The kit provided step-by-step instructions on how to run a file and included all relevant forms and information on how to obtain title and property searches. The owner of this kit business also set up the Conveyancing Society of Australia (CSA) as a separate entity.

To counteract this new way of handling a conveyancing transaction, some lawyers made life difficult for the brave consumer who was attempting to do their own conveyancing with a kit. However, this often did not sit well with the conveyancing clerk in charge of the file and they would assist the consumer in order to get the process done without delay or confusion.

Also established in the late 1970s was a franchising company which sold start-up conveyancing businesses to conveyancers who wished to go out on their own. The main incentive to purchasing a franchise was that it enabled a conveyancer to receive referrals straight away and be part of a strongly marketed brand so that they could earn an income quickly, as opposed to beginning a conveyancing business from scratch, relying on word of mouth to grow the business. The problem with the franchise arrangement soon became clear. The new franchisee received template documents which had been prepared by a solicitor. However, they were a 'one size fits all' solution that did not take into account the miriad of variables that can affect a file.

The VCA took a different approach and its philosophy was one of creating a professional association of highly experienced and educated members; the CSA was mostly made up of those people who were running conveyancing companies that were not members of the VCA. VCA did not wish to promote its members as doing cheap or low cost conveyancing but concentrated on promoting its members' professionalism and educational credentials.

Whilst Victorian conveyancers were attempting to organise themselves into a more cohesive group, New South Wales was going through similar issues and, after a very dark period for NSW conveyancers (see Chapter 5), a *Conveyancers Licensing Bill* was introduced into the NSW Parliament in 1992.

Buoyed by their win, representatives from the NSW conveyancing fraternity flew down to Melbourne and a meeting was arranged on 14 July 1992 with Victorian conveyancers from the three main groups to provide an update on the forthcoming NSW Bill and to provide their expertise on the question of whether or not Victoria should seek similar reforms and how these reforms could be achieved.

It was clear that there was a degree of friction between these three Victorian groups and the NSW conveyancers urged them to unify in working towards licensing in Victoria. A proposal to establish a Steering Committee was put forward and accepted which was made up of two members of each group and a meeting was arranged for later that month.

The first meeting of the Conveyancers' Steering Committee took place on 20 July 1992 at the Prahran Town Hall in Melbourne with over 100 conveyancers in attendance. The audience learned of the historical background of establishing conveyancing businesses in Victoria, after which a proposal was put forward to appoint a Task Force, whose first job was to organise a body to represent all conveyancers interested in licensing. It was emphasised that all conveyancers should be unified under one banner but, at that stage, there was no proposal for the separate bodies to merge. The audience was also urged to keep the meeting confidential to ensure that the LIV did not become aware of their activities.

The question of funding the campaign would need to be addressed and attendees were encouraged to spread the word in suburban and regional areas to ensure that the Steering Committee represented as many conveyancers as possible. It was also agreed that a Register of Victorian conveyancers should be compiled. A motion was put forward and passed unanimously to establish the Task Force which would be made up of the current Steering Committee members.

Over the next few months the Task Force met regularly to discuss the issues and to formulate a proposal to incorporate an association to represent conveyancers with the main purpose of lobbying the Victorian Government to introduce a licensing regime.

The proposed name for the organisation was the 'Australian Institute of Conveyancers (Victorian Division) Inc.' which was chosen to align the Victorian body with the national body of conveyancers which was being formed around this time.

At a meeting of Task Force members on 17 August 1992, the acceptance of the name was unanimous. However, it became clear that, for incorporation to work, the VCA would have to be absorbed into this new entity and refrain from its current activities. This proposal was put to a meeting of VCA members on 14 September 1992 and unanimously rejected. Despite the VCA being committed to the introduction of licensing for conveyancers in Victoria, members felt that the present Task Force appeared to have too many ideological differences to be workable. It felt that 'lawyer bashing' or anti-legal profession tactics, designed to denigrate the legal profession, would not assist the cause or lead to the Government favourably considering a licensing regime for conveyancers. The VCA considered that the way forward was to create higher standards of behaviour for the profession. Shortly after this meeting the VCA members who had served on the Task Force resigned.

The Task Force was therefore abandoned.

CHAPTER 5

THE NATIONAL CONVEYANCING PROFESSION

IN ORDER TO understand the emergence of the conveyancing profession throughout Australia, it is worth detailing the various paths which led to each jurisdiction establishing a representative body. Some, like New South Wales and Victoria had to fight to gain recognition as independent providers of conveyancing services by the introduction of regulation by their respective governments. Conveyancers in New Zealand also had a hard road to licensing.

South Australia

With the introduction of the Torrens System in South Australia in 1860 came the establishment of land brokers (see Chapter 1 – History of Conveyancing). However, it was not until 1973 that the Land Brokers' Society was formed. The earliest years of the Society coincided with the greatest threat to the land broking profession. Following pressure from lawyers who could see their income from conveyancing waning, the South Australian Government was considering introducing a *Legal Practitioners Bill* which would have limited the documents that land brokers were able to produce. The Society, with the support of the Real Estate Institute, gained exemptions for land brokers in the *Legal Practitioners Act 1981* (SA). Without the efforts of both organisations, land broking could have disappeared as a viable profession.

In 1994 a more efficient system of registration for conveyancers was introduced with the passing of the *Conveyancers Act 1994* (SA). This Act brought about the change of name from land broker to conveyancer.

Western Australia

In Western Australia property settlements were traditionally conducted by clerks working for law firms, real estate agents and banks. All representatives of the parties to a transaction would meet at the Land Titles Office and check all documents before settlement and registration.

In 1967 the first settlement agency was established in Western Australia and by 1970, with the emergence of more firms, the Association of Settlement Agents was formed. By 1972 the industry had grown to 30 agencies and the Law Society in Western Australia became concerned that there was no legislation governing settlement agents and instigated test cases to clarify the law. The settlement industry called a meeting and established a fighting fund to resist any Bill which proposed strong controls over the industry. An alternative Bill was devised by the settlement agents and, after intense lobbying, the *Settlement Agents Act 1981* (WA) was passed providing for the registration and control of settlement agents in Western Australia.[1]

Northern Territory

The emergence of licensed conveyancers in the Northern Territory was not as a result of a grass roots campaign by conveyancers, but

---

1 From AIC(WA) Website – August 2022.

came about due to a private member's Bill which was introduced into the Northern Territory Parliament amending the *Real Property Act*. The changes were minor but allowed anyone to set up a conveyancing business with no requirement to complete an educational course or to provide evidence of experience.

This immediately prompted conveyancers, who were mostly working in solicitors' offices, to make representations to their Attorney-General who stopped the changes and promptly introduced an amendment to the *Agents Licensing Act 1979* (NT) (the Act which regulates real estate agents) to include a section on specialist conveyancers with the Agents Licensing Board as the licensing authority. Licences began to issue in 1993 and existing conveyancers were grandfathered to allow them to set up conveyancing businesses.

New South Wales

New South Wales archival records disclose that personal property transfers occurred from the late 1790s but in fact conveyancers practised without any legal status or recognition during this time. In 1847, with the introduction of *The Taxation of Attorneys Bills of Costs Regulation Act* (NSW), certified conveyancers came into existence.

There were no more than 73 certified conveyancers practising in NSW up to the introduction of the *Legal Practitioners Bill* in 1935. This Bill provided that no further certificates would be issued for anyone to practise as a conveyancer and therefore the number declined over time. The Bill passed without any comment from the press or the conveyancers themselves. By 1967 the remaining conveyancers were granted unrestricted solicitors' certificates by the Law Society of NSW and all mention of conveyancers was deleted from the Act.

Conveyancing remained in the hands of solicitors until the 1980s and, although the Torrens system of property ownership had been introduced into NSW, land brokers were never introduced outside South Australia.

Similar to what was happening in Victoria, in 1989 a small group of unregulated practising conveyancers joined together to form the Association of Property Conveyancers in order to lobby the NSW Government to re-establish a regulatory system of licensing. Like Victoria, NSW conveyancers employed a solicitor to do the parts of the conveyancing transaction which were considered 'legal work'. There was strong opposition from the solicitors but, after much lobbying of parliamentarians, the profession gained recognition with the passing of the *Conveyancers Licensing Act 1992* (NSW). Initially conveyancers were limited to undertaking only small residential properties and regulatory control was in the hands of the Law Society of NSW but eventually the *Conveyancers Licensing Act 1995* (NSW) was passed, expanding the scope of work that licensed conveyancers could perform encompassing commercial and rural property and businesses. Control of the regulation of the profession was then passed from the Law Society to the Department of Fair Trading.[1]

The NSW Law Society was vehemently opposed to the increased scope of work for conveyancers but received no sympathy for its stand. An Australian Financial Review editorial of October 1995 suggested that it was *motivated by self-interested concern for the financial health of the average lawyer.*[2]

---

1 From AIC(NSW) – A Brief History of the NSW Conveyancing
   Profession by Dale Turner – 2001 – and a Brief History of Conveyancing
   in NSW by Alan West,CEO, in 2004.
2 Australian Financial Review Editorial – October 1995.

Tasmania

The *Conveyancing Act* was passed by the Tasmanian Government in 2004 and a few paralegals, who had been working for solicitors, were able to sit an examination to gain a licence to operate a conveyancing company.

Despite submissions made to the Tasmanian Government that the Act include the same wide definition of the scope of work that appeared in the NSW *Conveyancers Licensing Act 1995,* the Government opted for a definition of a conveyancer as –

> *'being a person who is not a legal practitioner and who carries on a business that involves the preparation for fee or reward of dealings within the meaning of the Lands Titles Act 1980 (Tas).'*

Australian Institute of Conveyancers

The Australian Institute of Conveyancers (AIC) was established in 1993, and incorporated under the *Associations Incorporation Act 1985* (SA). It was made up of members of the associations for conveyancers that had been established at that time in New South Wales, South Australia, Western Australia and Northern Territory, i.e. –

- The Land Brokers Society of South Australia, incorporated in 1978, became SA Division of the AIC.
- The Settlement Agents' Association, incorporated in 1979, became the WA Division of the AIC.
- The Association of Property Conveyancers Ltd, incorporated in 1989, became the NSW Division of the AIC.
- Legislation to enable conveyancers to be licensed in Northern Territory was introduced in 1993 and the Australian Institute of Conveyancers (Northern Territory) was quickly registered.
- Tasmania became a Division of the national body in 2004.

Since 1993 the Victorian Conveyancers Association (VCA) had worked towards becoming the Victorian Division of the national Australian Institute of Conveyancers. VCA representatives had been invited to attend regular National Council meetings in Adelaide as observers and had provided input into discussions on professional indemnity insurance, education, etc. However, because the national body was made up of the States where conveyancing licences existed, the majority of these States were reluctant to grant the VCA Division status, as they were not licensed and there was little possibility of becoming licensed in the foreseeable future. The VCA argued that it had set a benchmark for membership which reflected the same standards required for licensing, i.e. compulsory professional indemnity insurance, completion of a well accepted conveyancing course, completion of continuing professional development, etc. Finally the national body agreed and, following the unanimous vote by the VCA Committee on 6 May 1997, on 1 July 1997 it became a Division of AIC, and renamed Australian Institute of Conveyancers (Victorian Division) (AICVic).

AIC's vision was to create a national profession which would eventually include all States and Territories. The mobility of qualified professionals from jurisdiction to jurisdiction should be the right of any appropriately qualified Australian conveyancer and should include a scope of work which should be without limitation. Its vision was to foster, promote and advance the profession of conveyancers and to promote uniform educational and ethical standards.

Later in the 1990s the AIC was forced to change its structure because of a situation that arose in WA. It went from being made up of the members of the various State and Territory professional associations for conveyancers, to the actual Divisions being the members. The Constitution of AIC stipulated that to be a member a conveyancer had to be a member of one of its Divisions in NSW, SA, WA or NT. At the time there were three organisations in WA representing conveyancers. One conveyancer, who was a member of a group that was not the Division of AIC, complained to the Australian Competition and Consumer Commission (ACCC) arguing that the stipulation that he was obliged to belong to the Settlement Agents' Association in order to be part of the national body, was discriminatory. The ACCC then wrote to AIC in support of the WA conveyancer's claim. Urgent meetings of the National Council took place resulting in the AIC Constitution being changed to make the Divisions the members, not the individual conveyancers.

The AIC sits on various boards and working parties throughout Australia and participates in discussions and decisions not only pertaining to rules regarding licensing and education, but also to recommend any changes to laws and regulations.

Mutual Recognition and the Equivalence of Occupations

Despite the introduction of the *Mutual Recognition Act 1992* (Cth) and its adoption by all jurisdictions, conveyancers still faced considerable difficulty in gaining interstate reciprocal recognition because educational prerequisites for practice and the range of activities undertaken by conveyancers differed from one jurisdiction to another.

In 1997 the NSW Department of Fair Trading published '*Mutual Recognition of Conveyancers – a Discussion Paper*' which was based on the NSW Crown Solicitor's opinion which argued that –

- SA conveyancers are not equivalent to NSW conveyancers but can be made so with conditions.
- WA settlement agents and NT conveyancing agents are not the same occupations as NSW conveyancers and it was unlikely

that equivalence in respect of WA and NT occupations could be achieved by the imposition of conditions.

Eventually with the passing of the *Conveyancers Act 2006* in Victoria there was recognition that Victorian and NSW conveyancers were equivalent occupations.

Queensland

Although certified conveyancers had been operating in Queensland since the mid 1880s, in 1940 legislation[1] was introduced that prohibited any more certificates being issued, resulting in the remaining certified conveyancers being phased out by the 1980s.

In 1993 a well-established land broker from South Australia, Paul Sande, moved to Queensland and opened up a conveyancing company on the Gold Coast. Sande had worked for twelve years in the South Australian Land Titles Office and had been a land broker for nine years in South Australia. He applied to the Queensland Law Society for a Conveyancers' Practising Certificate to enable him to conduct land transactions in Queensland. The application was refused and Sande challenged the decision in the Administrative Appeals Court, but whilst he awaited the decision, he opened up a conveyancing business and began operating. Ultimately the Appeals Court rejected his application. Throughout 1994 he and his company were prosecuted by the Law Society under the *Queensland Law Society Act* for unlawful legal practice and convicted on numerous occasions.

Not to be dissuaded, Sande then turned his attention to the *Mutual Recognition Act 1992* (Cth) which provided that a licensing authority in one jurisdiction must grant a licence to a person who holds a licence in another State or Territory for an equivalent

1 The Queensland Solicitors' Conveyancing Reservation: Past and Future Development – Part 1 – Mark Byrne and Reid Mortensen

occupation. For mutual recognition to succeed there must be a mutual understanding of what are 'equivalent occupations'.

Sande made application under the *Mutual Recognition Act 1992* (Qld) for his South Australian licence to be recognised, arguing that the occupation of conveyancer existed in Queensland. The *Supreme Court Act 1867* expressly provided for the rights of a conveyancer to practise, subject to certain conditions. He argued that the *Legal Practitioners Amendment Act 1938* (Qld) did not abolish the occupation of conveyancer in Queensland. However, again his application was denied.

He then applied to the Special Minister for State, Garry Johns, who had raised Sande's case with COAG, but the Commonwealth received legal advice that resolution of the case would require significant change to the mutual recognition scheme, requiring recognition of 'activities' rather than 'registration'.

The Law Society of Queensland and its members subjected Sande to a long running campaign of intimidation and court appearances before he conceded defeat and moved over the border to operate in Tweed Heads in NSW where his SA licence was recognised. Eventually he returned to SA to practise.

The Australian Institute of Conveyancers (AIC) had been lobbying the Queensland Government since the mid 1990s to introduce a licensing system to comply with National competition Policy. In 2004 in response to the NCC,[1] the Queensland Government submitted that the Queensland market was already competitive and that the cost of regulating non-lawyer conveyancers ...*was likely to exceed the minimal benefits that lowering barriers to entry might bring.* The NCC disagreed and it was then up to the Queensland Government to provide a more convincing rationale for the argument.

---

1 National Competition Council – National Competition Policy Report (2005).

A lot of hard work and resources were devoted by AIC to the campaign (including a call to members to contribute to a fighting fund) and, for a time, it looked like it had the ear of the Queensland Attorney-General. A draft Bill had been drawn up to present to the Labor Cabinet. However, just before the presentation of the Bill, the Premier, Peter Beattie, called a snap election and the Bill was shelved. The Labor Party was returned to Government but the new Attorney-General, David Beanland, was vehemently opposed to the introduction of licensed conveyancers and the Bill did not succeed.

There had also been three trips by AIC Presidents to Queensland to meet with successive Attorneys-General but the argument that Queensland was not complying with NCP was continually refuted by the Government.

The next attempt to break the Queensland solicitors' monopoly came in the early 2000s when Dale Turner, a NSW licensed conveyancer and President of the NSW Division of AIC, applied to become a 'Solicitor with Conditions' in Queensland. He argued that there had been 'certified conveyancers' in Queensland since the introduction of the *Supreme Court Act 1867* (Qld) and therefore the occupation of conveyancer had existed. (In fact the *Legal Practitioners Act of 1938* (Qld) provided that no-one would be admitted to practice as a conveyancer after 1 January 1940. The number of conveyancers had therefore gradually diminished and the last certificate appears to have expired in 1987).

Despite the best efforts by Dale and his legal team, the Australian Administrative Tribunal rejected their arguments.

Queensland still prohibits conveyancers from operating independent conveyancing companies, despite the work of the Australian Institute of Conveyancers. The legal profession still maintains a strong monopoly over conveyancing work.

Australian Capital Territory

Like Queensland, the Australian Capital Territory has resisted the
idea of introducing licensed conveyancers. The Australian Institute
of Conveyancers has had meetings with the Government, arguing that NCP required the market to be opened up to licensed
conveyancers. However, to date, the Government has resisted the
proposal and the solicitors' monopoly continues.

New Zealand

There are similar parallels between Sande's campaign in
Queensland and the campaign fought by Lester Dempster in
New Zealand, including the fact that Dempster's professional
background was similar to Sande's. It included ten years with the
New Zealand Department of Lands and Survey and ten years as
Assistant Land Registrar of the Land Transfer Office. He also
established the New Zealand Society of Conveyancers.

Dempster applied to be licensed as a land broker in New
Zealand on three occasions in 1992 and twice in 1994.[1] On each
occasion he failed to satisfy the Registrar-General of Land that
he was appropriately qualified and experienced. In 1995 the High
Court granted an injunction upon application of the Auckland &
District Law Society (ADLS) restraining him from acting as a
solicitor. His appeal in 1997 to the High Court was refused.

Ironically, Lester Dempster was more successful in having his
qualifications recognised in Australia than in New Zealand. In
1996 he applied to the Northern Territory Agents Licensing Board
for a licence to carry on a business as a conveyancing agent in
Northern Territory. Notice of his application was published in the
newspapers in Australia and New Zealand and the only objection

---

1 The Conveyancing Debate Refocused by Peregrine Whalley – published in
   NZ Law Journal – March 1998.

lodged was by the Auckland & District Law Society (ADLS). The Agents Licensing Board dismissed the ADLS's objection and Dempster became the first New Zealander to obtain registration as a land broker/conveyancer under the *Trans Tasman Mutual Recognition Act 1997* (Cth). This action ultimately resulted in the New Zealand Registrar-General of Land in 1999 approving the registration of Dempster as a non-lawyer conveyancer based on his Australian conveyancing qualification.

After a long and bitter battle with the legal profession in New Zealand (and even the banks), the Government finally introduced the *Lawyers and Conveyancers Act 2006* (NZ) which regulated both lawyers and conveyancers. The Act came into operation on 1 August 2008 and paved the way for non-lawyer conveyancing specialists to operate in New Zealand. It also authorised the New Zealand Society of Conveyancers to have the sole responsibility for registration of conveyancers and the administration of the Act. The scope of work permitted was similar to the NSW *Conveyancers Licensing Act 1995*. Lester Dempster became President of the New Zealand Society of Conveyancers.

Sadly, Lester Dempster did not live to enjoy the benefits of the introduction of the Act and the establishment of a strong conveyancing profession in New Zealand as he died in 2009.

CHAPTER 6

THE PATH TO LICENSING – PARTS 1 & 2

PART 1

In October 1992 the Liberal-National Coalition won Government in Victoria and Jeff Kennett became Premier. Jan Wade became Attorney-General and lost no time in announcing a thorough review of the legal profession. The need for change had been prompted by the TPC's report and the Federal Government's Access to Justice Advisory Committee's recommendations which had been accepted by COAG, resulting in a nationwide shakeup of the legal profession.

A Working Party was established, chaired by Dr Greg Craven, which undertook a major overhaul of many aspects of the legal profession and recommended that –

- Instead of the LIV having a monopoly on the issuing of practising certificates, other bodies could do so, if they became Recognised Professional Associations (RPAs). (In the early 1990s the LIV devoted considerable time and effort to bring charges against lawyer, John Little, for the offence of not paying his fees to the LIV to obtain his practising certificate. He argued that it was similar to having to join a union, which he did not want to do. On 9 June 1994 he was interviewed on *ABC Radio* where he mentioned the Government's discussion paper and, in particular, the proposal that this monopoly should be removed from the LIV. He warned, however, that the proposed Legal Practice Board (LPB) could delegate regulatory powers to the LIV, thereby putting them in a stronger position due to the massive resources accumulated over time.)[1]

- A Legal Ombudsman to handle complaints be appointed. The existing situation where the LIV investigated its own members had raised conflict of interest accusations, for example, the case of Stan Rosenberg (Chapter 2) where it took the LIV six years to bring him to trial.

- The removal of control of the Solicitors Guarantee Fund from the LIV. This was the fidelity fund that compensated victims of solicitor fraud.

- The LPB would oversee the profession and become the Regulator.

The LIV accepted that it was time that its role in the handling of complaints against solicitors ceased, thereby removing the accusation of conflict of interest, but it was not prepared to agree to the other changes without a fight, and with its vast resources, consultants were employed to lobby State Members of Parliament to try and overturn Jan Wade's plans. The LIV had a couple of recommendations of its own, however, which were designed to comply with competition policy such as being allowed to incorporate, to form limited liability partnerships and to allow contingency fees.

The VCA determined that the review was an important opportunity to increase pressure on the Government to introduce a licensing scheme for conveyancers.

Since incorporation in 1991 the VCA had steadily increased its membership, initially restricting its members to those who

---

1   This warning was prescient in view of what happened in 2005 – See Chapter 9 – Law Institute of Victoria v Maric & Anor.

were Fellows of the paralegal organisation, the Institute of Legal Executives (ILE), but later expanding the criteria for membership to those who had met certain specified educational and experience criteria but were not necessarily members of the ILE. Its Committee met fortnightly and consisted of a number of strong minded conveyancers, most of whom were also running their own businesses. All Committee work was carried out voluntarily after hours or at weekends whilst the group worked tirelessly to build a viable profession, setting high standards of education and behaviour for members. It was not until the mid 1990s that resources allowed for the employment of an administrative assistant two days a week to support the work of the Committee.

A significant part of the VCA Code of Conduct was that conveyancers should undertake Continuing Professional Development (CPD) and complete a specified amount of training annually, thereby providing evidence of the campaign to set high standards for the industry. In working towards this goal, it was necessary for VCA to develop a targeted training program, holding regular seminars, workshops and State conferences with speakers well versed in property law and procedures. These well attended events provided an opportunity for city, regional and interstate professionals to catch up with colleagues in a more social environment.

One speaker who became a regular was lawyer Simon Libbis, a well-known property law specialist. In mid 1994 the LIV held a property law seminar with Simon as its main speaker. Normally such events would be confined to solicitors but the event came to the attention of some conveyancers who registered, expecting their cheques to be returned and registration refused. This did not happen and the event took place with a number of VCA members in the audience. After the seminar Simon was approached and asked if he would give a similar presentation to a group of conveyancers at a VCA event later in the year. He agreed, much to the derision of, and threatening behaviour by, his colleagues. He made it clear that he would give the presentation as a private consultant and not as a representative of the LIV. Simon went on to provide the VCA and its members with many training events on the law and practices around property, and conveyancers benefitted enormously. Simon has written a number of well received books focussing on conveyancing (in conjunction with AICVic Members Sandra Murphy and Joan Lentini). He became part of Electronic Conveyancing Victoria before becoming Registrar of Titles in South Australia and eventually headed up the National Electronic Conveyancing Office (NECO).

After consideration of the Victorian Government's review, the VCA lodged a submission calling for licensing of conveyancers and the removal of the prohibition on them undertaking 'legal work'. In due course meetings were held with representatives of the Department of Justice (DOJ) where the VCA's case was laid out.

In September 1994, DOJ advised that the Working Party was finalising the framework of the Bill but had not turned its attention to conveyancers. VCA doubled down on its lobbying but unfortunately, by the end of 1994, a spokesperson from DOJ advised that the Victorian Government was not in favour of licensing or even certification. The justification for this decision was –

- It was too cumbersome and expensive.
- None of the reports to Government actually recommended such action.
- It was anti free trade.
- The Government did not want to restrict entry to the people wanting to operate conveyancing companies.

The Government believed that the current system was working well and it did not see a compelling reason to change. Jeff Kennett was a strong proponent of privatisation and deregulation and was not persuaded, even though other States had introduced licensing systems. The DOJ had canvassed the opinions of the LIV, the Land Titles Office and Consumer Affairs Victoria (but not the VCA) and had formed the opinion that there was no evidence of major problems. LIV members were in a good position because they were still employed to undertake the legal work in a conveyancing transaction, thereby making conveyancers beholden to them.

The VCA wrote to the Government restating the problems associated with the current lack of regulations which included –

- The fact that many conveyancing companies ran trust accounts, which were not regulated or audited. (VCA discouraged its members from running trust accounts).
- Without legislation conveyancers could not obtain meaningful fidelity insurance.
- The public had no way of knowing the competence, experience and honesty of individual conveyancers.
- There was no compulsory professional indemnity insurance.
- The current position was extremely unsatisfactory and a potential scandal could erupt at any time (see Chapter 7 – The Grove Disaster).

The review and subsequent report of the Working Party took a few years to emerge but in it the VCA was acknowledged as the peak body for conveyancers in Victoria. When the Bill to reform the legal profession was finally introduced into the Victorian Parliament, it had certainly remodelled the legal profession, however the conveyancing industry was extremely disappointed to discover that only four pages of the over three hundred page *Legal Practice Bill* was devoted to the regulation of conveyancers.

One Victorian Minister confidentially stated that the review of the legal profession had taken such a long time to complete, that the Government had no appetite to launch a further investigation into whether or not conveyancers should be licensed. Instead the question would be left to the new Legal Ombudsman to investigate any anti-competitive behaviour and make recommendations to the Government.

The Bill recognised the occupation of 'conveyancer' but still did not allow conveyancers to undertake 'legal work'.

The most glaring omission was that the Government saw no necessity for a conveyancer to hold compulsory professional indemnity insurance cover. The Act merely required that if a conveyancer held professional indemnity cover, then they were required to notify their client.

S.330(1) of the *Legal Practice Act 1996 (Vic)* stated –

'Conveyancers are required to –
– set out in a statement, in a form approved by the Board, whether or not the conveyancer holds insurance which covers them against civil liability for their conveyancing work. This statement must be on all public documents …. and must be in a conspicuous place outside the conveyancer's office.' (The wording approved by the Board for inclusion on public documents was either – 'this firm holds professional indemnity insurance against civil liability; or this firm does not hold professional indemnity insurance.')

S.330(2) and *Practice Act* stated –

'Conveyancers are also required to –
– give all prospective clients a written notice setting out whether the conveyancer holds such insurance and, if so, the amount of insurance cover and any relevant exclusion or limitation. The written notice must also include the details of any legal practitioner retained to perform the legal work, and if no such legal practitioner is regained, prospective clients must be advised that the conveyancer is not entitled to perform legal work'

(i.e. the preparation of any document that creates, varies, transfers or extinguishes an interest inland; or the giving of legal advice).

Whilst the fact that conveyancers could not undertake legal work was a major issue, it was also felt that the requirements in relation to the disclosure of professional indemnity cover was unreasonable. No other profession was required to make such disclosures. This was interpreted as another example of a Board (mainly made up of lawyers) which had been set up to control lawyers, also controlling conveyancers.

Despite numerous submissions to the Government prior to the introduction of the *Legal Practice Act 1996 (Vic)(Practice Act)*, it still did not consider that professional indemnity cover should be mandatory for all conveyancers. It was left to the consumer to read and understand this information when it was shown to them. From the VCA's point of view this was completely unsatisfactory and, following discussions with AON Professional Services (AON), an insurance broker involved in finding cover for VCA members, a submission was made to the LPB supported by AON, requesting two amendments to the *Practice Act* –

- That professional indemnity insurance cover be made compulsory for all conveyancers. (A minimum of $500,000 was recommended, although VCA members held $1million cover.)
- That S.330(2)(a)(ii) be deleted, i.e. disclosing the amount of the professional indemnity cover.

The submission said in part –

'The very fact that we have a deregulated market in Victoria for conveyancers makes it even more important that the public is protected from inexperienced and unqualified people. This

protection should include mandatory professional indemnity cover for all conveyancers.'

It was also argued that the requirement to disclose the amount of cover to clients was unnecessary and discriminatory. No other profession had that requirement imposed on them. AON supported the VCA's argument and pointed out that *to disclose the amount of cover (indemnity) available to a third party would not only result in an increase in the level of litigation, but also inflate claims brought against practitioners.*

Although the submission was acknowledged by the LPB, no further action was taken to amend the *Practice Act* at that stage.

The *Practice Act* finally received Royal Assent, coming into operation on 1 July 1997, introducing a number of reforms which significantly changed the way the legal profession was regulated and, to a limited degree, conveyancers.

On 1 July 1997 the VCA became a Division of the Australian Institute of Conveyancers, and changed its name to the Australian Institute of Conveyancers (Victorian Division) (AICVic). (See Chapter 5 – National Profession)

Finally, in May 1999 the LPB advised that it would support the AICVic's request for S.330(2)(a)(ii) to be removed from the *Practice Act*, i.e. the requirement to disclose the amount of professional indemnity cover held. It indicated that any change to introduce compulsory cover for all conveyancers would involve a number of policy issues to be addressed and AICVic was encouraged to direct the request to the Government (which of course they had).

The Path to Licensing Continues

Over the next few years, AICVic concentrated on expanding its influence with various Government departments, in particular the

Land Titles Office and the State Revenue Office. It conducted training sessions with high profile speakers on areas of property law which were open to both members and non-members. The AICVic was held in high regard by Government and other organisations and was considered the 'go to place' for conveyancing information and became a defacto hotline for members of the public with queries and complaints. This service was achieved despite only having the resources to employ part-time staff.

After the disappointment of the Victorian Government rejecting the arguments for licensing, the AICVic turned its attention to its Certified Practising Conveyancer (CPC) program. They established it as a membership category, with a view to using it as a catalyst to develop a 'certification program' to be submitted to Government as an alternative to licensing. It was argued that a AICVic CPC member, who had passed a set criteria of educational qualifications, experience and held professional indemnity insurance, should be allowed to undertake the 'legal work' component of a conveyancing transaction.

Although the *Practice Act* had completely changed the regulation of lawyers, the LIV continued to use its strength and influence to undermine the conveyancing industry. It repeatedly wrote to the solicitor retained by AICVic to assist its members comply with the Act, querying their arrangements. It was strongly believed that this was a conflict of interest, because lawyers were competing in the same marketplace as conveyancers and the LIV should not be allowed to investigate conveyancing businesses.

In April 1997 the Professional Standards Department of the LIV wrote to the AICVic requesting an explanation as to the procedure members followed in relation to the legal work that was required to be undertaken by a legal practitioner. AICVIc's response was to ask under what delegation or authority was the LIV operating in order to make these enquiries. The LIV responded saying that it received many complaints about conveyancers and was required to monitor instances of unqualified legal practice under S.314 of the *Practice Act*. The correspondence went on to remind conveyancers that it could seek an injunction at any time against individuals breaching that Section of the *Practice Act*.

AICVic immediately sent a letter to the LPB objecting to the unnecessary approaches of the LIV. The LPB assured AICVic that the LIV did not have express powers of investigation in respect of non-lawyers but conceded that it did have a role in relation to 'unqualified practice'. The LIV's interpretation of unqualified practice and that of AICVic was clearly in dispute.

The pressure from the LIV became so significant that a complaint was sent to the new Legal Ombudsman, Kate Hammond who agreed to investigate. The behaviour was also drawn to the attention of Bill Robinson, the then Chief Executive Officer of the LPB.

In August 1999 the Victorian Government introduced changes to the *Sale of Land Act 1962* (Vic) resulting in the inclusion of a number of disclosures and warranties in the contract of sale. AICVic was frustrated that it had not been consulted in relation to these changes, as independent conveyancers made up a large component of the industry. The changes meant it was even more important that the Government allow conveyancers to provide their clients with 'legal advice' before they signed a contract of sale.

The Development of Electronic Conveyancing Victoria (ECV)

In 1999, Victoria's Land Registry introduced an initiative in relation to electronic conveyancing. AICVic was invited to attend a meeting on 24 August where the Electronic Conveyancing

Project was established. The meeting was called by the Registrar of Titles, Rosalyn Hunt, and attended by Land Registry staff and representatives of the Law Institute. The Project became known as Electronic Conveyancing Victoria (ECV) which proposed making the conveyancing/settlement/lodging process more efficient and to reduce paperwork by using the internet. The Project was not meant to capture 100% of all transactions into Land Registry, but would be designed to capture 60%.

Some areas that would need to be addressed were –

- The parties involved in the system would need to be identified by a trusted identifying provider who would need to be readily accessible to both city and regional areas, such as Australia Post.
- The vendor of the property would need to provide their practitioner with supporting evidence of their right to sell, i.e. passport, driver's licence, rate certificate, etc.
- An online workspace would be created by the vendor's representative with all relevant information inserted once a contract was signed. The purchaser's representative would then insert all their client's information as well as mortgage details.
- This workspace would be continually updated by the parties.
- Once settlement date and time were fixed, the parties would meet online and, after documents were approved, the funds would be transferred electronically in a few seconds, following which the documents would be automatically lodged for registration with Land Registry.
- Stamp duty would be paid separately by Electronic Funds Transfer.

It was an ambitious Project and all involved acknowledged that there would be initial teething problems and that it would take years of consultation to develop. However, the consensus was that the Project was worth pursuing.

PART 2

In October 1999, the Liberal/National Coalition was swept from power and the Labor Party, led by Steve Bracks, won Government. Rob Hulls became the Attorney-General and indicated that he wished to undertake further reform of the legal profession.

By August 2000 AICVic was buoyed by the news that Hulls was reviewing the *Legal Practice Act 1996* (Vic). In his Media Release of 9 June 2000 he stated –

> *'There has been significant public and professional disquiet about the operation of the existing regulatory system. It is far too complex and cumbersome...We want a regulatory system that is clear, effective and accessible and that has the confidence of the public and the profession.'*[1]

The review was to be conducted by Professor Peter Sallmann, Crown Counsel, and Mr. Richard Wright, Associate Director of the *Civil Justice Review Project* and they were to report back to the Attorney-General by December 2000.

Disappointingly there was no mention of conveyancers in the terms of reference. However, the review presented AICVic with another opportunity to argue for licensing and that suitably qualified conveyancers should be able to undertake the legal work involved in a transaction.

The idea of employing a consultant to assist in the preparation of a submission to the review was approved by the Committee and the former Registrar of Titles, Rosalyn Hunt, was approached. Ms Hunt was willing to be involved and proposed Jude Wallace, a respected lawyer experienced in policy and research, was also

---

1 Rob Hulls Media Release – 9 June 2000.

willing to be involved in trying to achieve a separate regulatory regime for conveyancers. Some of the issues raised were –

- Should the push be for licensing as opposed to accreditation, bearing in mind NCP and the costs involved in establishing a licensing regime?
- The need to ensure that the eventual regulation was no more restrictive than what existed at the time.
- It was essential to ensure that the LIV had no control over conveyancers.[1]
- Any legislation needed to adopt the 'legal work' definition which appeared in the NSW *Conveyancers Licensing Act 1995*. This would provide a wide-ranging definition of the sort of work that conveyancers could undertake. Section 4 of the NSW Act defined Conveyancing Work as –

  '(1) For the purposes of this Act, conveyancing work is legal work carried out in connection with any transaction that creates, varies, transfers or extinguishes a legal or equitable interest in any real or personal property, such as (for example) any of the following transactions –

  (a) a sale or lease of land,

  (b) the sale of a business (including the sale of goodwill and stock-in-trade), whether or not a sale or lease of land or any other transaction involving land is involved,

  (c) the grant of a mortgage or other charge.

  (2) Without limiting subsection (1), conveyancing work includes –

---

1 When the NSW *Conveyancers Licensing Act 1992* was introduced, the Regulator was a body made up of a majority of lawyers, which proved to be unworkable. In due course the Department of Fair Trading became the Regulator of NSW conveyancers.

(a) *legal work involved in preparing any document (such as an agreement, conveyance, transfer, lease or mortgage) that is necessary to give effect to any such transaction, and*

(b) *legal work (such as the giving of advice or the preparation, perusal, exchange or registration of documents) that is consequential or ancillary to any such transaction, and*

(c) *any other legal work that is prescribed by the regulations as constituting conveyancing work for the purposes of this Act.'*

A NSW Supreme Court case reinforced the argument that one could not compartmentalise a conveyancing transaction into non-legal work and legal work. The case related to a struck off solicitor who had given an undertaking to the Supreme Court that he would not act as a solicitor. However, he continued to act as a conveyancer and the Law Society of NSW took him to Court, arguing that he was still 'acting as a solicitor'. When the Court unravelled his work, it considered that the work he was undertaking as a conveyancer could not be divided from that undertaken by a solicitor – it was all legal work – and he was therefore holding himself out to be a solicitor.[1]

Around this time AICVic received a call from a Policy Officer on behalf of the LPB who advised that it had been receiving complaints from the LIV about conveyancers and also about a disbarred solicitor who had been acting as a conveyancer. At the request of the Attorney-General, the LPB had been instructed to look at some form of regulation for conveyancers. A copy of the AICVic Code of Conduct and CPC Programme were provided immediately.

In due course, representatives from AICVic were invited to meet the LPB's Chief Executive Officer, Bill Robinson, and his colleagues to discuss the review of the *Practice Act*. Whilst they were

---

1 *Anthony Hart v NSW Law Society 1989-90.*

told that their initiatives to reform the conveyancing industry were laudable, the LPB did not believe that licensing of conveyancers was on the Government's agenda. This was once again disappointing news. However, the LPB said it would support AICVic's submission in principle and would submit, in its response to the review, that a licensing system should be set up for conveyancers and that professional indemnity insurance be made compulsory.

Electronic Conveyancing Victoria (ECV) Continues

During 2000, an AICVic representative attended monthly meetings of the Electronic Conveyancing Project (ECV), which initially envisaged that the system would be comprehensive and cover every part of the conveyancing process from preparing a vendor's statement, a contract of sale, final settlement and lodgment and everything in between.

By October 2000 the Project's IT team had produced a vendor's statement online which allowed a practitioner to key in data with appropriate information and to automatically include searches of the title and plan and to access a Land Information certificate online. Eventually it was anticipated that all property certificates would be available online, but this was dependent on all local Councils coming on board.

In December 2000, at a media event at Land Registry, which was designed to give the EC Project some publicity, a journalist queried if once all settlements were electronic, the cost to the consumer would be less. This idea, a complete fallacy, seemed to be taking hold in Government circles, but in time it proved to be wishful thinking.

By the end of 2000 Rosalyn Hunt and Jude Wallace had prepared a comprehensive submission, again putting forward AICVIc's proposal for the introduction of a licensing scheme for conveyancers. The submission was sent to the Attorney-General with a copy to the LPB.

AICVic was also involved in a review of the Conveyancing Industry Competency Standards which were the basis for conveyancing courses, and by early 2001 the new standards were set to go to the State Training Board for approval to become the basis of any conveyancing course taught by a Registered Training Organisation.

From early 2001 mid 2003 AICVic took every opportunity to bring their arguments into the public domain and to try to convince the Victorian Government that conveyancers should be licensed and permitted to undertake the legal work component of a conveyancing transaction.

By July 2003 the Government had developed certain amendments to the *Practice Act* which were due to go before the Victorian Parliament in the autumn session of 2004. The LPB again invited AICVic representatives to a meeting to discuss the proposed amendments, seeing it as a good opportunity to try and introduce some small changes for the conveyancing industry. A full and frank discussion took place where AICVic stated that, at the very least, it was imperative that the Government make it mandatory for all conveyancers to carry a prescribed minimum level of professional indemnity cover of $1 million. The LPB could give no guarantees, but wanted to be ready to move quickly if the Government indicated that it was prepared to include some further regulation of conveyancers in the *Practice Act*.

National Competition Council

The NCC had been established in 1995 as a result of the passing of the *Competition Policy Reform Act* following agreement by the Commonwealth, State and Territory Governments. It is a statutory authority that functions as an independent advisory body for all governments on the implementation of national competition reforms.

As previously mentioned, the NCC required the States and Territories to review legislation to identify anti-competitive behaviour and to open up competition in certain areas, including the legal profession. They were required to introduce legislative reform to overcome these restrictions and those States and Territories who undertook such reviews and complied with the NCC requirements could receive substantial payments from the Commonwealth Government.[1]

In its 2002/2003 Report the NCC listed a number of outstanding issues and stated –

'While considerable progress has been made in reviewing and reforming legislation that contains restrictions on competition, issues remain in areas such as... professional regulation.'[2]

However, in the NCC's 2003/2004 report it expressed its concern with the lack of progress, especially in relation to opening up the legal profession to competition.

In August 2003 AICVic was contacted by the NCC which was finalising a report to the Federal Government. It was seeking information about conveyancing in Victoria and AICVic explained that the anti-competitive situation still existed for Victorian conveyancers, of which they were not aware. The NCC had been advised by the Victorian Government that it was reviewing the *Practice Act*, but were unaware that the review did not encompass

---

1 The Tasmanian Government was swift to introduce licensing for conveyancers in 2004, thus ensuring it received payments and avoided penalties. Ironically, Queensland did not undertake an open review of its legal profession but it is understood still received payments.
2 National Competition Council Report of 2002/2003

conveyancers and that the Attorney-General had confirmed he would not be reviewing this area. [1]

Media Support

By the end of 2003, AICVic and its national colleagues were in regular contact with the nation's leading newspapers and kept journalists informed as to what was happening in Victoria, comparing our situation with that of the other licensed States.

One journalist in particular was keen to publish articles exposing the injustice of the situation for conveyancers in Victoria who were not allowed to operate in the same way as their counterparts in NSW, SA, WA and NT. Chris Merritt was Legal Editor of the Australian Financial Review (AFR) and contacted AICVic to advise that he had seen a briefing paper to be presented to a meeting in Hobart of the Standing Council of Attorneys General (SCAG) regarding the reservation of legal work and consistency of the legal profession nationally. The Law Council had written to the Attorney-Generals stating that one of the areas to be reserved to the legal profession should be –

'The creation, extinguishment, transfer of legal or equitable interests in real property.'

The National AIC lost no time in writing to SCAG opposing the adoption of such a proposal, arguing –

---

1 Ironically, in a speech to economists (which was reported by Shane Wright in The Age newspaper on 17 October 2022) the new Federal Competition Minister, Andrew Leigh, signalled a new wave of competition reform, supported by incentive payments to the States. He believed that Australia needed a 'good dose of competition', arguing for a return to the Hilmer reforms of the 1990s and 2000s. Almost $6 billion was paid to various governments over more than ten years under these reforms.

*'that it would see the occupation of conveyancer diminished or
revert to being the domain of legal practitioners only. Such a suggestion flies in the face of legislation that exists in NSW, SA, WA
and NT which license conveyancers and enable them to provide
direct competition to legal practitioners in that area.'*

It also pointed out the untenable situation that existed for
conveyancers in Victoria, Queensland and Tasmania, calling for
an end to the legal profession's monopoly. *'The Attorneys General
should not cave in to the Law Council's proposals but ensure that competition is enhanced.'*[1]

Thankfully, the Attorneys General rejected the Law Council's
proposal.

Professional Indemnity Insurance and the Electronic Conveyancing Project

During 2003 there had been considerable advancement in the work
being done on the Electronic Conveyancing Project. However,
one of the impediments were the rules to be introduced to regulate those who would access the electronic system, i.e. solicitors,
conveyancers, banks. The basic requirement was that these par-
ticipants would have to hold a minimum amount of professional
indemnity insurance cover, as not all conveyancers operating in
Victoria had this cover and with no mandatory requirement nor
appropriate regulation in place, this could present a major hurdle
to the Project.

By early 2004 it was clear that AICVic needed to take more
control of the professional indemnity insurance situation and
enquiries were made with brokers to see if a better combined policy
could be arranged for members which would include some fidelity

---

1   Letter from AIC to SCAG – November 2003.

cover. AICVic wanted the Government to see that all AICVic members held a $1 million minimum amount of cover plus some fidelity cover. The policy would be monitored by AICVic to ensure all policies were current.

Eventually a broker firm, Rowland House, was able to negotiate an acceptable policy through underwriter, Ace Insurance. In due course, the AICVic combined policy attracted about 120 members and was maintained through Rowland House. When licensing was introduced on 1 July 2008, the policy was made redundant.

The Lobbying Continues

In early 2004, Geoff Craige, a previous Minister in the Kennett Government who was now working as a lobbyist, was approached to assist AICVic with the push to get the Victorian Government to change its mind. Geoff urged AICVic members to talk publicly about the current unfair conditions under which conveyancers operated and undertook to discuss the situation with Members of Parliament that he was confident would listen.

The Introduction of Title Insurance into Australia

In February 2004, AICVic was approached by a Title Insurance company who wished to market this new type of property insurance to its members. Title Insurance had originated in the United States of America[1] where it had become the backbone of a property transfer in that country. The principle was that a property

1 In the early 1800s private insurers entered the market in some States of the USA offering insurance against defective titles. The industry expanded significantly after the Second World War, largely in response to the demand for title guarantees by providers of credit. Title insurance protects the buyer and lender from financial loss in the event that there are problems with the title to a property.

purchaser took out this type of insurance before settlement, and would then be covered for unexpected issues that arose whilst they owned the property, such as illegal structures and fences erected on incorrect boundaries.

One of the concerning aspects of this type of insurance was that it was being presented as eliminating the need to obtain property certificates and make proper investigations. AICVic's initial reaction was that it could not recommend this type of insurance, as it would diminish the conveyancer's role and contradicted good conveyancing practice which was to obtain a full set of property certificates on a file to ensure that there were no notices, orders or issues that may affect a purchaser's future enjoyment of a property.

Eventually only two title insurers became established in Australia – *Stewart Title* and *First Title*. Both companies learned quickly that take up amongst conveyancers would be low to non-existent if they were advocating that there was no need to obtain property certificates and undertake due diligence. However, the other aspects of the insurance were worthwhile and both title insurance companies have established a significant share of the market.

The Electronic Conveyancing Project Continues

On 16 March 2004, AICVic was invited to attend a press conference at Land Registry held by the Minister for Planning, Mary Delahunty, to launch the *Transfer of Land Amendment Bill* which was about to be introduced into the Victorian Parliament. The main purpose of the Bill was to amend the *Transfer of Land Act 1958* to empower the Registrar to require verification of identity of all parties to a transaction before registering an instrument. It also defined the words 'electronic instrument' and 'electronic lodgment network'.

An AICVic representative was invited to give a presentation on the merits of electronic conveyancing and the Land Registry was able to demonstrate a mock settlement to the media. The invitation to speak showed that the Land Registry now considered AICVic an important stakeholder in the Project.

A Vendor's Statement – Legal Opinion Sought

During the early 2000s a disturbing trend was emerging whereby the vendor's statement pursuant to S.32 of the *Sale of Land Act 1962* (Vic) *(the Act)* was expanded to not only include the prescribed information set out in the Act, but also to include additional terms, conditions, warranties, etc., some of which had contractual connotations. An example of such a condition was one which stipulated that a purchaser would be penalised by the vendor imposing a substantial fee if settlement was delayed due to the purchaser's actions.

The *Sargeants* franchise supported this trend in an effort to provide uniform documentation to its franchisees, eliminating the need for them to use their own judgment as to what should or should not be included in a contract of sale. These template S.32s statements (which were designed by *Sargeants'* solicitor) were regarded by AICVic and many legal practitioners as breaching the basic rules for the preparation of a S.32 statement, namely that the vendor's statement was merely a prescribed statement by the vendor and should not introduce wording which would impose contractual obligations on the purchaser.

There were differing opinions as to whether or not it was possible to include extraneous material such as notices, special conditions and warranties in a S.32 Statement. For example, Russell Cocks, a well-known property law commentator held the opinion that –

> *'the vendor's statement forms part of the contract between the parties and any special condition in the vendor's statement are binding.'*

Conversely, Robert Forrest, a solicitor working at the LIV, stated –

> *'The practice of purporting to include special conditions into a contract by means of clauses in a S.32 statement is a highly questionable one. There are no known court judgments on this issue. However, basic contract law and the underlying purpose for which S.32 Sale of Land Act as enacted, would indicate that a court or tribunal would not view favourably a party seeking to rely on these type of special conditions.'*

In 2003, to clarify these divergent opinions, AICVic obtained written legal opinion from Barrister P.N. Wikrama, QC as to the validity or otherwise of such practices. Wikrama's report referred to the Second Reading Speech of the Attorney-General at the time when the disclosure statement came into existence via a Bill amending the *Sale of Land Act 1962* (Vic) to include S.32. The Attorney-General said –

> *'The second substantial change to conveyancing practice affected by the Bill is to provide for the principle of caveat vendor, that is, that vendors of land are under an obligation to supply sufficient information relating to the property to a purchaser prior to obtaining the signature to a contract of sale. Under the present law, the conveyancing proceeds on the principle of caveat emptor, that is, the onus is placed on the purchaser to make his own searches concerning the property in question. Furthermore, there is no obligation upon a vendor to provide any information except as to latent defects of title or quality, if the purchaser does not seek it.'*

Wikrama's view was that S.32 was designed to provide certain information before the purchaser signed a contract of sale which would be essential to enable the purchaser to make an informed decision as to whether or not to enter into the contract and that any matters in special conditions or warranties which were included in the vendor's statement would not, in their present form, automatically become included in the contract of sale. However, his opinion was that a contract can refer to another document that already exists incorporating that document into the contract, so that they can be read together. This is known as the 'connected documents' rule. It would therefore be necessary to set out in the contract the fact that the S.32 statement contained terms and conditions which were to be incorporated by agreement into the contract of sale.

This legal opinion was distributed to AICVic members with a warning that the practice was fraught and that the information required under S.32 of *the Act* to be included in a vendor's statement should be adhered to and the practice of including additional terms and conditions abandoned.

This legal question became important later when a member of AICVic was challenged by the LIV as 'engaging in legal practice' by including 'representations and warranties' in a S.32 statement (see Chapter 9 – *Law Institute of Victoria v Maric*).

The Lobbying Continues

Meanwhile in May, Geoff Craige, lobbyist and former Victorian Minister, reported that he had spoken to a number of Parliamentarians and there appeared to be no major objections to licensing of conveyancers, but ultimately it would be Rob Hulls' decision.

In June, AICVic representatives attended a meeting at Consumer Affairs Victoria (CAV) to discuss the amount of complaints it was receiving about conveyancers and to provide a clearer picture of the issue. CAV did not appear to have received the large number of complaints that AICVic received. A possible reason for this was that most consumers hadn't taken the time to lodge a formal written complaint to CAV, as required. Over the years, AICVic had received numerous complaints about conveyancers which had been documented as evidence of the types of issues that were arising. Where these complaints were about its members, efforts were made to resolve the issue promptly to prevent the matter escalating. However, complaints about non-members were forwarded to CAV for action. CAV advised that it did not have the resources to handle these complaints but agreed to report on the substance of the meeting to Dr David Cousins, the Director of CAV.

Meanwhile in early June 2004, the Tasmanian Government passed legislation to introduce licensed conveyancers to comply with NCP requirements. The national AIC Council had had some meetings with the Tasmanian Government during the consultation period and encouraged it to ensure that the definition of 'conveyancing work' in the proposed Act mirrored the definition contained in the NSW *Conveyancers Licensing Act 1995*. The NSW definition was also a fundamental part of the AICVic proposal for any legislation designed for Victorian conveyancers. The final legislation, however, did not include the definitions that AIC had recommended, but stipulated that Tasmanian conveyancers could only prepare documents within the meaning of the *Land Titles Act 1980* (Tas).

AICVic distributed a press release to Victorian Members of Parliament advising of this new Tasmanian legislation, calling on them to support the abolition of the lawyer's monopoly in Victoria, which elicited many positive responses. At a meeting later that month with Andrew Mackintosh, the Shadow Attorney-General, he declared that he was sympathetic to AICVic's problems and agreed to try and raise support for a licensing regime.

Around this time there were rumours that the Government was beginning to seriously consider some form of regulation for conveyancers. It was clear that the LIV would endeavour to influence any such legislation but few lawyers were as vocal against conveyancers as Peter Mericka. In an article published in the Law Institute Journal (LIJ) in July 2004 he asserted that –

'Conveyancers in Victoria regularly engaged in unqualified practice ... When a conveyancer is approached by a vendor of real estate for what is commonly regarded as "conveyancing", before the execution of a binding contract of sale, the conveyancer invariably engages in legal practice.'

He also decried the use by conveyancers of 'supervising solicitors', equating it to an advertising ploy and concluded by saying that –

'Regulators have been reluctant to require compliance with the Legal Practice Act with the result that unqualified legal practice in this industry is the norm.'[1]

In August 2004 the LIJ published a response to Mericka's article from the AICVic's President, Pauline Barrow, in which she outlined that the intention of the Working Party which advised the Government in relation to the introduction of the *Practice Act*, was to ensure compliance with NCP to accommodate conveyancers. She cited advice from the Executive Director of the NCC, John Feil, in November 2003 to all Governments that conveyancing practice restrictions were a significant impediment to increased competition in the legal profession and confirming that he had written to the Victorian Department of Treasury and Finance (DTF) noting that such restrictions should be removed in accordance with best practice across Australia.[2] Ms Barrow

---

1 Law Institute Journal July 2004 – article by Peter Mericka.
2 Letter from National Competition Council to Department of Treasury and Finance – 6 July 2004.

went on to clarify that under the *Practice Act,* conveyancers were not required to have a 'supervising solicitor' as Mericka suggested, but must advise their client of the name and address of the legal practitioner they retain …. The Working Party in its report states – '*Conveyancers fulfil an important role by creating competition in the market… this role should be maintained and should not be impaired.*'

At a meeting with Land Registry on 8 July regarding the rules for the introduction of electronic conveyancing, AICVic was assured that the Parliamentary Council did not want current industry players excluded from the EC Project because of an issue with professional indemnity insurance. Barbara Flett, the Registrar of Titles at the time, understood that the EC Project could not introduce rules that a substantial number of conveyancers could not comply with, i.e. they could obtain $1 million of professional indemnity insurance cover but fidelity cover or run off were problematic.[1]

The momentum was starting to build for a licensing regime to fix this problem and pressure was mounting on the Victorian Government.

Later in the month at a meeting with representatives of the Attorney-General's Department, AICVic expressed great concern that the *Practice Act* was about to be abolished and replaced with the *Legal Profession Act 2004* (Vic)(*Profession Act)* but conveyancers had not been consulted. The Attorney-General's Department had appointed Price Waterhouse to undertake the review of the *Practice Act* and it had recommended that the conveyancing question should be the subject of a further review because it was too complex for a 'quick fix'. The DTF was keen to have the review proceed and

---

1 Run off meant that former licensees who had sold their practice or simply ceased operating were covered for claims for seven years after the sale or closure. This ensured that the consumer had a right of recourse against an insurance policy should a claim arise.

assurances were received that the Attorney-General would consult the Minister for Consumer Affairs, about such a review.

On 31 August, AICVic representatives attended a meeting with John Lenders, Minister for Consumer Affairs and reiterated the problems experienced by conveyancers with respect to professional indemnity insurance, fidelity cover and the prohibition on undertaking legal work, which was an essential part of a conveyancing transaction. The Minister felt that it was too difficult to introduce a licensing scheme but undertook to consult Dr Cousins and Dr Clair Noone of his Department.

Following this meeting, discussions were had with Chris Merritt of the AFR who requested copies of the various submissions that had sent to the Government, which informed an article published on 17 September 2004.[1]

At a meeting a week later with the Registrar of Titles, Barbara Flett, and Deputy Registrar, John Barry, they advised AICVic that the Land Registry had appointed an insurance consultant to look at the professional indemnity issue – LIV were insisting on a level playing field for lawyers and conveyancers – i.e. $1 million cover, fidelity and run off.

A trigger was needed to convince the Victorian Government to change its mind about licensing conveyancers. It came in the form of the Grove Conveyancing Services disaster.

---

1 Australian Financial Review article by Katherine Towers – 17 September 2004.

CHAPTER 7

THE GROVE DISASTER

GROVE CONVEYANCING SERVICES (Grove) was established in Geelong in 1988 by Bob Day, with his brother, Geoff Day, joining as an employee. In 1990 Alanna Boston, wife of Geelong Solicitor, Philip Boston, joined as a partner. Bob built up a solid reputation as a trustworthy local businessman running an efficient conveyancing business and Grove had branch offices in Apollo Bay, (where Bob and his wife had a holiday home), and at Werribee.

Geelong was booming, due to the waterfront re-development, the widening of the Geelong Road and the Avalon Airport expansion. Property conveyancing was busy and lucrative.

On 21 October 2004, AICVic received notification from a member based in Geelong advising that Grove had closed its doors. The Geelong Independent Newspaper published an article advising that staff were out on the street and detectives had been called in to investigate the firm.[1] AICVic began to receive letters and distressed calls from members of the public complaining about Grove's lack of response to queries. As the owner was not a member of AICVic, these complaints were referred to CAV.

---

1 Geelong Independent Newspaper – 21 October 2004.

Something was amiss with Grove and, once cases of fraud started to be exposed, the Police were called in around October 2004. Alanna Boston denied she had any involvement in the day-to-day management of the business. The LIV investigated Boston Lawyers' books but were satisfied that the firm had no involvement in the Grove matter.

Grove's collapse was the third major financial disaster to hit Geelong within a fifteen year period. The Pyramid Building Society collapsed in 1990 with debts in excess of $2 billion followed by the fraud committed by former mayor, Frank De Stefano, who had operated an accountancy business from which he stole approximately $8 million from clients. In March 2003 he was sentenced to ten years' imprisonment. Several people who had lost big sums of money in Pyramid had also been caught up in the Grove crash.

Clients impacted by this worrying situation demanded that the Police charge someone but in an article by Paul Heinrichs in The Sunday Age on 14 November 2004, he reported that the Detectives had indicated that the investigation, which was being carried out in conjunction with the major fraud squad and forensic accountants, would take 12 months to two years to complete, as they combed through thousands of files.[1] The firm was unable to account for clients' monies which it had received in the form of settlement funds, stamp duty and registration fees. Regrettably, the firm did not hold professional indemnity insurance or contribute to a fidelity fund, neither of which were compulsory for conveyancers.

AICVic immediately contacted the media, including the AFR and the Geelong Advertiser, reinforcing that it had been warning the Victorian Government for years about the lack

---

1 The Sunday Age – article by Paul Heinrichs 14 November 2004.

of regulation of conveyancers and alerting Government and Members of Parliament to the consequences.

It emerged later that Bob Day had a gambling addiction and the temptation of access to large amounts of money passing through his firm's accounts was too much to withstand. Many of his clients had sold their homes and re-invested their money through Grove. They had trusted him to hold onto their titles but later it was revealed that he had used those titles for collateral or had transferred them to other parties. Bob Day assured his clients that he would hold their money in a trust account but, due to the lack of regulation of conveyancers, such trust accounts were not audited.

The Grove disaster attracted considerable media attention and there was great concern expressed by the public. It became the trigger for the Victorian Government to finally take action and, on 10 November 2004, it announced the terms of reference for a review of the regulation of the Victorian conveyancing industry.

On 1 November 2004, representatives from AICVic met the Director of CVA and his staff to discuss the catastrophe, but emerged from the meeting disappointed with the lack of urgency on the part of CAV, considering that conservative estimates at the time were that Bob and Geoff Day had absconded with approximately $6 – $9 million of clients' monies!

In December 2004, Bob Day was declared bankrupt. The Bankruptcy Trustee, Phillip McGibbon of accounting firm Jenkins, Peake & Co, said that creditors would only receive approximately 10c in every dollar owed by Grove, but this was later recalculated down to less than 5c in the dollar, if anything.

CAV issued a media release in January 2005 advising consumers who may have been affected by the Grove collapse to contact them. The Department had seized approximately 15,000 files from the firm and was provided with assistance from the Land Registry staff to deal with the complexity of a conveyancing file.

The impact of the Grove collapse on other conveyancing businesses in the Geelong area was catastrophic, not to mention the negative publicity which had affected the industry more broadly. Not surprisingly, the legal fraternity used this opportunity to criticize conveyancing businesses and engender disquiet amongst consumers. John Cain Jnr, the Chief Executive Officer of the LIV, warned the public about putting their trust in conveyancing companies which were unregulated. He also criticized members of the public for using conveyancers instead of solicitors.[1] Ironically, the LIV were now calling on the Victorian Government to look closely at regulating conveyancers, but it was still not advocating that conveyancers should be able to undertake 'legal work.'[2]

It wasn't until June 2008 that Bob Day was finally charged with 293 counts of theft and deception relating to the loss of more than $12 million of clients' funds. He appeared in the Geelong Magistrates' Court on 12 June 2008, pleaded guilty and was sentenced to eleven years' gaol.

Geoff Day admitted to stealing from the company and pleaded guilty to 12 counts of theft, totalling $4.2 million. He was sentenced to eight and a half years' gaol.

AICVic believed that the Grove collapse could have been prevented, had its warnings over many years concerning the lack of regulation not been ignored. Surely now the Victorian Government would urgently introduce appropriate legislation?

---

1 Article in Law Institute Journal by John Cain Jnr – November 2004.
2 Australian Financial Review – comment by Chris Dale, President LIV –
   29 October 2004.

CHAPTER 8

THE PATH TO LICENSING – PART 3

THE FALLOUT FROM the Grove collapse was challenging for the industry but it was buoyed by a rumour in November 2004 that CAV was about to undertake a review of the conveyancing industry. It was frustrating to learn that the review would only be carried out internally by various Government departments and would not be an open and transparent review to which AICVic, and other stakeholders, could have input.

Co-incidentally, the NCC contacted AICVic again to provide an update on progress. The NCC was not aware of the CAV review but advised that its Assessment Report, which would be available in 2-3 months, would require the Government to remove the restriction on competition. To avoid complying with these directions, the Government would have to prove that the restrictions were 'in the public interest'.

There was friction between CAV and the Attorney-General's office – a source in the office of the Minister for Consumer Affairs advised that there was no agreement on how the review was to proceed or who was to fund it. The issue had now fallen into the lap of CAV due to the Grove situation and it would now have to deal with these issues.

On 16 November 2004, the *Legal Profession Bill* (*Profession Bill*) was introduced into the Victorian Parliament. The purpose of the Bill was to improve the regulation of the legal profession by implementing model provisions to facilitate the regulation of legal practices at a national level and to repeal the *Practice Act*. The Legal Ombudsman, Kate Hammond, was to be replaced by the Legal Services Commissioner. Ms Hammond had had a hostile relationship with the LIV and believed –

> *'that the new system would work only with a strong Legal Services Commissioner prepared to stare down professional associations such as the Law Institute of Victoria and the Victorian Bar.'*[1]

The new legislation meant that prosecuting power could be delegated to those associations, which could undermine the independence of the system. The LSB would oversee the profession, but Ms Hammond believed that it would be put under pressure to delegate power to those bodies to run investigations and prosecutions.

The Attorney-General, Rob Hulls, had dismissed her concerns but, as reported in Chapter 9, those powers were used by the LIV against its competitors.

The section in the *Practice Act* relating to conveyancers and conveyancing businesses was replicated in the new *Profession Act*, except for a slight change in wording, but the Act still did not require conveyancers to hold professional indemnity insurance, and the prohibition on undertaking legal work remained.

By the end of 2004, in discussions with the Registrar of Titles, Barbara Flett, AICVic made it clear that the introduction of the *Profession Bill* was a backward step for the conveyancing industry, as it did nothing to alter the lack of regulation, such as requiring mandatory professional indemnity insurance, fidelity and run-off,

---

1 Australian Financial Review article – 5 November 2004.

and this could jeopardise the conveyancers' participation in the EC Project. AICVic urged her to approach CAV to plead its case.

In November 2004 the Victorian Government finally announced a review of conveyancing regulation and *Allen Consulting Group (Allen)* was commissioned to conduct the review. The Minister for Consumer Affairs, John Lenders, said –

> *'consumers needed to have confidence in the conveyancing industry and any new regulatory regime should protect home-owners while not forcing up costs by over-regulation.'*[1]

Chris Merritt's article in the AFR on 10 December 2004 supported AICVic's argument of the need for a strong regulatory regime for conveyancers to enable them to participate in the EC Project. He commented –

> *'Even if the state government's inquiry into the regulation of non-lawyer conveyancers decides to remove the last restrictions on these people, another barrier may be about to descend... For several years, Land Victoria has been working on a plan to trans-form conveyancing by introducing a new electronic system that would do away with archaic settlement procedures. Non-lawyer conveyancers have been involved in discussions about the new system but they now fear they might be excluded just as the plan is nearing its final stages... Conveyancers' fears have been triggered by the emerging debate over what sort of consumer protection conditions will need to be imposed upon those who want to use the new system. Professional indemnity insurance and fidelity cover are among the conditions on the table – which sounds perfectly reasonable... But there's a catch. At the moment Victoria's non-lawyer conveyancers are subject to minimal regulation ...'*

---

1 Australian Financial Review article by Chris Merritt – 12 November 2004.

The writer was quoted as saying –

'that the absence of licensing has made it impossible for convey-ancers to obtain fidelity cover from the insurance market.'

The article concludes –

'And that might just be enough to ensure that solicitors who par-ticipate in the fast new world of electronic conveyancing would face minimal competition from non-lawyers.'[1]

In January 2005, following a reshuffle of portfolios, the Premier announced that John Lenders was no longer the Minister responsible for Consumer Affairs and that the portfolio had been taken over by Marsha Thompson, the Minister for Small Business and IT.

Allen Consulting Group

Finally there was to be an open review of the conveyancing industry and it was essential for AICVic to use every effort to convince the Government to introduce legislation on its terms. The Committee therefore decided that it needed the services of a lobbyist with an ear to Government and contacted David White of *Hawker Britten*. He had been a Minister in the previous Labor Government and was therefore well-connected and also interested in our situation and prepared to assist.

When AICVic representatives were invited to attend a meeting with Martin Stokie of Allen Consulting Group (Allen), discussion took place on a range of issues including the 'legal work' prohibition on conveyancers. AICVic wanted parity with NSW conveyancers and for the Government to comply with NCP and to stop the existing restrictive practices and emphasised that it had introduced a professional indemnity insurance

---

1 Australian Financial Review article by Chris Merritt – 10 December 2004.

policy for members, as well as having established a comprehensive conveyancing course through RMIT. Stokie raised the issue of whether proposals for the introduction of electronic conveyancing in Victoria provided justification for the introduction of a more comprehensive regulatory scheme. AICVic responded that whilst there may be an increased risk of fraud, electronic conveyancing would present further opportunities for gate-keeping and audit. Stokie proposed publishing a discussion paper which would put forward a range of regulatory frameworks, ranging from a mere register of conveyancers to a full licensing system and everything in between.

In early March AICVic met with the REIV to discuss regulation for conveyancers. REIV was now supportive of licensing but warned against being regulated through CAV. It reported that there was little transparency regarding complaints and they did not learn the details of such complaints until some 18 months after the event had taken place. As a result an agent could continue to breach the rules.

Word was received that the LPB was reluctant to amend the *Profession Bill* because it was based on the proposed national model for the legal profession, which was slowly being established. The irony was that most other States had their own separate conveyancing Acts. AICVic was warned by various sources that if separate legislation was introduced by the Government for conveyancers, it may not get all it wanted initially but it would be better to fight to get whatever it could in the legislation and, if some areas were not satisfactory, then work to get the Act amended later. Removing the restriction on conveyancers handling sale of business transactions and undertaking mandatory CPD were examples of areas that might not be agreed to initially by the Government, but could be negotiated once the Act had been introduced.

On 16 March, the Chief Executive Officer of the LIV, John Cain Jnr, invited AICVic representatives to a meeting at the LIV offices. Despite his comments in the LIJ article in early 2005 where he called the conveyancing profession *'unregulated amateurs'*,[1] they approached the meeting with a positive attitude, hoping that the LIV would now be more accepting. John Cain Jnr confirmed that the LIV was now agreeable to regulation for conveyancers but did not understand how a person could be qualified to undertake this work unless they had done a law degree. He appeared unaware of the RMIT conveyancing course and the range of property law subjects it covered. He did not agree that a conveyancer could handle subdivisions, multi-storey developments with bodies corporate etc., even if they had completed a dedicated course and had years of relevant experience in the area. There appeared to be no common ground that would enable the parties to move forward.

In April, Allen published its discussion paper. The Government had appointed a Steering Committee made up of representatives from DOJ, CAV and the DTF. At a meeting around this time between Dr David Cousins of CAV and the Registrar of Titles, the Registrar reinforced the view that the EC Project would fail if conveyancers were not licensed, and the Victorian Government was at risk of wasting a substantial sum on the Project.

The AICVic submission to the Allen discussion paper was a well-researched and comprehensive paper canvassing all the issues and correcting some of the misrepresentations that had appeared in the paper about conveyancing and how the industry in general operated. AICVic supported the removal of the legislative distinction of legal work and non-legal work in conveyancing, because these distinctions were anachronistic and anti-competitive and

---

1 Law Institute Journal article by John Cain Jnr – early 2005.

put Victorian conveyancers at a disadvantage compared with other States where conveyancers operated under a licensing scheme. AICVic confirmed that its members were qualified, competent and well educated and trained in their area of expertise, i.e. conveyancing. However, it did not support increased regulation of conveyancers if it meant no change to the definition of legal work.

In response to the discussion paper, the LIV submitted that it supported a comprehensive regulatory regime for conveyancers with mandatory professional indemnity insurance and fidelity cover, adequate training, etc, all under the control of CAV, but, not surprisingly, it continued to support the restriction on conveyancers undertaking legal work.

At a meeting with lobbyist David White, he was given a copy of the AICVic's response to the Allen paper. He was due to have a meeting the following week with an adviser to Rob Hulls and would gauge his thinking on the review. AICVIc mentioned that it had had discussions with the NCC and had been advised that the Council had sent a letter to the DTF recommending that the restriction on conveyancers undertaking legal work be removed. DTF had responded by saying that the conveyancing practice restriction would be considered in the context of the review of the *Practice Act*. The NCC confirmed this information to AICVic via a letter dated 6 July 2004.[1] David was delighted with the letter and said it was 'worth its weight in gold'.

During August AICVic followed up repeatedly with the DOJ to ascertain if the Steering Committee had received the Allen report, expressing its concern that the soon to be enacted *Profession Act* now contained a definition of 'legal services' which, it felt, would provide more ammunition to the LIV to take action against

---

1 Letter from NCC dated 6 July 2004 confirming earlier letter to Dept. Of Treasury and Finance

conveyancers. The Government did not believe that the wording of the Act would affect conveyancers and disregarded its concerns.

What came next shocked the profession and caused AICVic members many months of distress and uncertainty. In September 2005, the LIV served a Summons on AICVic member, Lydia Maric, setting out its intention to seek an injunction to restrain her from 'engaging in legal practice.'

CHAPTER 9

LAW INSTITUTE OF VICTORIA v MARIC

WHO WAS LYDIA Maric and why did she attract the ire of the LIV?

Ms Maric was an experienced conveyancer who had worked for solicitors since 1983 and had gained a significant amount of knowledge in this area of the law. Since 1994 she had been employed by solicitor, Anthony Sammassimo at *A1 Conveyancing Services*. With the emergence of conveyancing businesses in the late 1980s, a number of solicitors, in a bid to compete in the market, had set up separate conveyancing businesses, running alongside their legal practices.

In 1999, Ms Maric purchased *Home Conveyancing & Probate Services* from the legal firm *Home Wilkinson & Lowry*. Anthony Sammasimo's wife was also part-owner of the business and Mr. Sammasimo became the retained solicitor to the firm in order that Ms Maric could comply with the *Practice Act*. A few years later Ms Maric took control of the business entirely. All Probate matters were referred to another solicitor.

In September 2004, the LIV received correspondence from Messrs. Feltham Lawyers of Shepparton, Victoria, complaining about a S.32 statement which had been prepared by *Home Conveyancing & Probate Services* of Reservoir. Feltham's main issue was *that the S.32 contained clauses which appeared to be contractual terms which are normally included in a Contract of Sale of real estate.*[1] The so-called 'contractual terms' were inserted in the S.32 under the heading 'Representations and Warranties'. The complaint was also referred to the LPB which was responsible for the regulation of the *Practice Act*.

The LPB wrote to Ms Maric advising her that she should remove the word 'Probate' from the firm's name – which she did. She also advised the LPB that she was now using the AICVic S32 template, which did not contain Representations and Warranties. The LPB decided not to prosecute her for any perceived breach of S.314 of the *Practice Act* (prohibition on unqualified legal practice) in relation to the 'Representations and Warranties' contained in the S.32 statement that she had prepared and which had been the subject of Feltham Lawyers' complaint.

Under S.299 of the *Practice Act*, the LIV as a Recognised Professional Association (RPA) had the power, like the LPB, to take action against those who it determined were breaching the Act. Despite the fact that the LPB had declined to take further action against Ms Maric, the LIV were not satisfied with that response, as it had formed the view that by preparing the S.32 statement in question in the course of the conduct of a conveyancing business, that she and her firm were engaging in unqualified legal practice in breach of S.314 of the *Practice Act*.

The source of these 'Representations and Warranties' originated from a software package that Ms Maric inherited when she purchased the business from *Home Wilkinson & Lowry*. The package was known as *'Safeguard Solutions Computer System'* and was widely used by both solicitors and conveyancers. The package

---

1 Feltham's letter to the Law Institute of Victoria – September 2004.

assisted with the day-to-day administrative work of the business and contained forms and precedents which had been first approved by *Home Wilkinson & Lowry* (now HWLE).

Ms Maric had prepared the S.32 statement and then sent copies to the estate agent instructed to sell the property, accompanied by a letter instructing the agent to allow the vendor to read the S.32 statement carefully to ensure the information was accurate before it was signed and attached to a contract of sale. The letter also noted at the foot of the page that the firm employed Anthony Sammassimo for all legal work and that the firm held professional indemnity insurance against civil liability in compliance with the *Practice Act*.

In September 2005, Ms Maric was served with a Summons by the LIV setting out its intention to apply to the Supreme Court, the highest Court in Victoria, for an injunction to restrain her from 'engaging in legal practice'. The LIV believed she had done this by preparing a S.32 statement containing contractual terms.

This action was a shock to Ms Maric, the AICVIc and all conveyancers running conveyancing firms. The AICVic Committee was concerned at the implications and complexities of this application to the Supreme Court for an injunction against one of its members.

Prompted by Feltham's complaint, (and possibly by representations from some of its members, including Peter Mericka who had published an article in the LIJ in 2004 accusing conveyancers of engaging in unqualified practice),[1] John Mazaris of the Professional Standards Department of the LIV had written to Ms Maric on 22 September 2004, (12 months prior to applying for the injunction), seeking an explanation for her activities concerning the preparation of the particular S.32 statement and the business

---

1 Law Institute Journal article by Peter Mericka – 2004.

activities of her firm.[1] Ms Maric responded on 4 October 2005 confirming that all probate matters were referred to a solicitor and that the firm employed another solicitor for all legal work. She confirmed her belief that a S.32 statement was not a legal document but stated that she did not hold herself out to be a solicitor or to mislead the public in believing that she was a solicitor.

Subsequently, on 9 February 2005 Mazaris wrote again to Ms Maric, warning her that he had formed the view that she had engaged in unqualified legal practice in breach of S.314 of the *Practice Act* and, by its own motion, the LIV could seek an injunction against her preventing any such breach in the future. The LIV's delay in taking action was that it was waiting on the LPB to make a decision whether or not to prosecute Ms Maric.

The implications of an injunction being granted against a Victorian conveyancer, restraining her from preparing S.32 statements, would be devastating to all conveyancing businesses in Victoria and the AICVic resolved to support its member in winning this argument. AICVic took control of the case and funded it, with the proviso that it would be reimbursed once it won the case. Ms Maric agreed and AICVIc's Solicitor, Michael Benjamin, arranged for well-known Barrister, Nimal Wikrama QC, to represent her in Court.

The hearing took place in the Supreme Court on 16 September 2005 before Justice Hansen, who acknowledged the injunction that the LIV sought was not only from Ms Maric engaging in legal practice, but also that she be restrained from preparing any vendor's statements pursuant to S.32 of the *Sale of Land Act 1962 (Vic)*. The LIV, represented by Martin Randall, put forward the argument that by including Representations and

1 Affidavit of John Thomas Mazaris dated 31 August 2005.

Warranties in the S.32 Statement, Ms Maric had 'engaged in legal practice' and had undertaken legal work in breach of S.316 of the *Practice Act.*

Wikrama, on behalf of Ms Maric and her firm, argued that what she had done was 'conveyancing work' and, according to the *Practice Act*, this was defined as work other than legal work and that legal work was defined as the preparation of any document that creates, varies, transfers or extinguishes an interest in land. He submitted that the mere preparation of a S.32 statement did not involve engaging in legal practice within the meaning of the *Practice Act* and foreshadowed dire consequences would follow to the business of Ms Maric if the injunction were granted.

Unfortunately, despite Wikrama putting up a credible argument, the Judge granted an interlocutory injunction restraining Ms Maric from preparing S.32 statements, pending a trial anticipated later in the year.

Wikrama was able to convince Judge Hansen, however, that the LIV should provide an undertaking for damages because, if the Judge in the subsequent trial determined that Ms Maric did not have a case to answer, then she should be compensated. On the basis of this undertaking by the LIV, the Judge granted the interlocutory Injunction.

The profession was shell-shocked by this outcome and the implications of the injunction for all conveyancers; would the LIV begin to pick off conveyancers one by one and apply for further injunctions?

How does a conveyancer practise when prevented from preparing S.32 statements, which are a significant part of a conveyancing transaction? Ms Maric was aided by solicitor, Michael Benjamin, but this required travelling from Greenvale to *Michael Benjamin & Assoc* in Dingley each week, a 120km round trip, so that he could prepare the S.32 statements for her clients. The ramifications of this obligation were enormous, not only in terms of the financial impact which threatened the viability of her business, but also in terms of the personal implications which affected her reputation around the area. The costs associated with having S.32s prepared by a solicitor meant in reality that there would be little point in a client engaging a conveyancing firm, as the fees charged would bring them closer to the fees charged by a solicitor.

The granting of the injunction prompted AICVic to accelerate its lobbying, beginning with letters to the Attorney-General, Rob Hulls, the LPB, CAV as well as Members of Parliament, expressing outrage that the LIV had taken this unwarranted action.

Chris Merritt, who was now writing for The Australian newspaper, was kept abreast of the situation and began a series of articles supporting AICVic's stand. The AFR wrote supporting articles.

At the same time a couple of significant events were anticipated. The new *Legal Profession Act 2004* (Vic) (*Profession Act*), which had been working its way through Parliament, would finally be enacted on 12 December 2005. The *Profession Act* introduced a range of reforms to the legal profession (these changes were raised in the subsequent trial and became significant). The second event was the report of *Allen Consulting Group* in relation to the review undertaken of the conveyancing profession. A report had gone to the Government's Steering Committee, but progress was slow.

AICVic wrote to Sue Walpole of the LPB requesting confirmation that the LPB had delegated authority to LIV to take Court action against Ms Maric. The Board responded as follows –

'The Board provides global rather than case by case funding to the LIV. It has no power to prevent the LIV from undertaking Court action pursuant to S.316 of the Legal Practice Act 1996. As you

know I did attempt to dissuade the Chief Executive Officer of the
LIV from commencing the action against Ms Maric.'[1]

On 12 October 2005 Rob Hulls' office was again contacted and AICVic was told that the Attorney-General understood their frustration in the delay in publishing the Allen report, but that the recommendations contained in that report needed to be signed off by a number of departments and each had to report on how any changes would affect them. The Attorney-General was certainly abreast of the court case and understood the urgency of a resolution.

Following the Interlocutory Order, the full hearing of the case was due to take place on 30 November 2005 and, after some research and much discussion, it was decided to employ the services of a well-respected QC, Greg Garde, to run the case, with Michael Roberts appointed as his Junior. (Greg Garde went on to become president of the Victorian Civil and Administrative Tribunal (VCAT) and later became a Supreme Court Judge.) Nimal Wikrama was also involved. Also supporting the Barristers was Michael Benjamin as instructing solicitor and his part-time researcher, George Madden, a former Victorian Crown Solicitor. The AICVic was represented at all meetings by its President at the time, Pauline Barrow, and Chief Executive Officer Jillean Ludwell (the writer) as well as Ms Maric. The national AIC expressed its full support for AICVic and used its influence to garner support.

So confident was the LIV in taking this action that it appeared to ignore the fact that the Victorian Government had already commissioned the *Allen Consulting Group* to undertake a review of conveyancing. The terms of reference of the review stated that the Government was looking to remove the restriction on

---

1 Letter from Legal Practice Board after October 2005 re Court action.

conveyancers undertaking legal work. The LIV intended to convince the Government to disallow such a proposal by asking the Supreme Court to make a judgment on the legal work question.

At the initial meeting with the Barristers, it was suggested that the most expedient way to remove the injunction was to draw a line in the sand and advise the Judge that the S.32 statement with which the LIV had issue, was prepared before Ms Maric became a member of AICVic and she had since stopped using the form contained in the Safeguard package and was using the AICVic template, which adhered to the requirements of S.32 of the *Sale of Land Act 1962* (Vic). However, after some discussion it was agreed that this argument would not prevent the LIV from taking action against more conveyancers and it was critical that it was proven that a S.32 statement was not legal work, and certainly not a legally binding document.

The legal team began gathering as much information as possible to refute any arguments that could be raised at the forthcoming trial, including investigating whether or not the LIV had the authority to take action against the Defendants. The LPB would have had to delegate that authority because once the *Profession Act* replaced the *Practice Act* on 12 December 2005, the power of the LIV as a Registered Professional Association expired. This point would be significant later.

To ensure that members were abreast of the case and the implications for their businesses if the LIV succeeded, a meeting was held which was addressed by AICVic's solicitor, Michael Benjamin. He reinforced the reality that the action taken against Ms Maric could have been taken against any conveyancer running a business. Members were encouraged to contact their local Member of Parliament and express their concerns. All members attending supported the AICVic's action in supporting Ms Maric and the profession in general.

At a LIV Council meeting the forthcoming trial was discussed and the members were adamant that they did not wish to lose the argument that legal work should be quarantined to solicitors. The LIV was apparently not aware that Ms Maric was a member of the AICVic (and had been since 15 November 2004). A number of conveyancers had already been referred to the LIV by its members complaining that they were undertaking legal work or holding themselves out to be a solicitor.

Contact was made with the Federal Parliamentary Secretary responsible for competition policy to advise that the Victorian Government had not complied with NCP and complaining that the NCC had allowed the LIV to maintain its monopoly against conveyancers. What was really frustrating was that the NCC had already provided payment to the Victorian Government on the promise that it would remove the solicitor monopoly.

On 26 October 2005, AICVic received confirmation from the Attorney-General's office that the Allen report had been received and only needed to be signed off by Rob Hulls and Marsha Thompson, the Minister for Consumer Affairs.

AICVic contacted the Secretary of the DTF expressing frustration at the delay in publishing the Allen report but also expressing anger that the Victorian Government had already received the NCC payments to remove the monopoly. Meetings were also held with Opposition Members of Parliament to put forward AICVic's arguments, some of whom were sympathetic.

In November the Committee of AICVic resolved unanimously to strike a levy of $500 for each member to accumulate a fighting fund to pay for the Barristers' fees for the upcoming trial. The overall majority understood the dire situation that all conveyancers faced and supported payment of the levy.

On 30 November 2005, the the Law Institute of Victoria v Maric & Anor. began in Court 9 of the Supreme Court with

Justice Osborn presiding. The Defendants were Ms Maric and her firm, *Home Conveyancing Reservoir*, represented by Greg Garde QC, Michael Roberts and Nimal Wikrama QC. The LIV, the Plaintiff, was represented by Mark Dreyfus QC (currently Federal Attorney-General) and Martin Randall.

Dreyfus opened the hearing by putting forward the argument that the injunction had been sought to protect the public from unqualified people engaging in legal practice. He used similar arguments that had been raised at the initial court hearing, i.e. that the S.32 Statement that the Defendant had prepared was 'legal work' and she had breached s.316 of the *Practice Act*.[1]

Greg Garde in turn put forward the argument that Part 13 of the *Practice Act* introduced the definition of 'conveyancer', i.e. being a person who carries on a business, in the course of which conveyancing work is carried out directly or indirectly for fee or reward. A further concept was that conveyancing work was defined as 'other than legal work' carried out in connection with the transfer or conveyance of a freehold or leasehold interest in land. Legal work was confined to the preparation of any document that creates, varies, transfers or extinguishes an interest in land or the giving of legal advice. Under the *Practice Act*, a conveyancer had two choices when it came to legal work –

- To pay a legal practitioner to perform the legal work in connection with any particular transaction; or
- To simply indicate to a client that they were not authorised to perform legal work.

Part 13 had therefore been introduced into the *Practice Act* in order to provide guidance to conveyancers as to how conveyancing businesses could legally operate.

---

1 Transcript of Court hearing of 16 September 2000.

Garde then went on to point out that a S.32 statement was not a document which creates, varies, transfers or extinguishes an interest in land and, therefore, the S.32 statement that the Defendant had prepared did not fall foul of the concept of legal work, as defined in the Act. Nor did Ms Maric give the client legal advice in any way, shape or form. The S.32 statements were sent to the estate agent which was normal practice. The *Practice Act* gave recognition to the need for increased competition in the area of conveyancing brought about by the changes to the *Trade Practices Act 1962* (Cth), which opened up the legal profession to competition designed to benefit the consumer.

Garde said that the core business of what a conveyancer does includes the preparation of information or documents such as a S.32 statement which is an information document – it is a business activity that is authorised under Part 13 of the *Practice Act,* which had been in operation for nearly a decade. He also cited the case of Felman v Law Institute of Victoria (1998) 4VR324, where Kenny J. had referred to a passage in a judgment handed down in Cornall v Nagle (1995) 2VR188 which found that accountants and other professionals may give opinions on questions of mixed fact and law falling within their expertise, and acknowledging the lawful pursuit of an occupation of advising on a matter within a person's expertise.[1]

Judge Osborn commented – *In other words Part 13 recognises the occupation of conveyancer* – Greg Garde responded – *Yes this is so.*

Garde went on to provide an outline of the Defendant's work experience, her education in property law and the sequence of events in relation to her ultimately owning *Home Conveyancing Reservoir.* He alluded to her Affidavit which pointed out the ramifications if the Court was to hold that she was required to tender

---

1 Transcript of Court hearing of 30 November 2005.

all S.32 statements to a solicitor (which was exactly what she had been obliged to do since the temporary injunction had been granted to the LIV). Those ramifications would be serious and would affect the viability of her business and the costs involved would mean in reality that there would be no point in a client engaging a conveyancing firm as the fees would not be less than the fees charged by a solicitor.

Ms Maric had already completed part of a conveyancing course through RMIT and an Affidavit was produced from Joanne Mackay, a Lecturer at that University, setting out the substance of the training for conveyancers which included S.32 statements. Even the CAV website in 2004 referred to S.32 statements being prepared by the seller's solicitor or conveyancer prior to a sale.

Since joining the AICVic, Ms Maric had used the S.32 precedent which had been prepared by Michael Benjamin & Associates for use by its members and therefore there was no need for any ongoing injunction to restrain her.

Day 2 of the hearing took place on 1 December 2005, with the Plaintiff's Barrister arguing that the majority of the Affidavits produced by the Defendant were irrelevant. Greg Garde argued that these Affidavits were entirely relevant – the Defendant's Affidavit detailed her experience and education, as well as details of her acquisition of the original business which included the Safeguard software package. In addition, he said that the Affidavit by solicitor, Anthony Sammassimo confirmed his approval of the documents that the Defendant used and that he was the retained solicitor for the business.

His Honour accepted Greg Garde's submissions and said –

'It seems to me that it does set out background matters. It does depose to approval of the system adopted by the company and it does depose to an actual practice of referring matters for legal

*advice to a solicitor… They're relevant to the way the Defendants
put their case.'*

His Honour also accepted an Affidavit deposed by Joanne
Mackay, as it bore on the Defendants' case, i.e. that you may have
an occupation which is not a legal practice but where some actions
are legitimate but may not constitute legal practice. Judge Osborn
went on to say –

*'it seems to me that this Affidavit seeks to establish that there is in
fact an occupation of conveyancer.'*

A further Affidavit was sworn by AICVic President, Pauline
Barrow, explaining the origins of the organisation and its role in
the development of the conveyancing profession. She advised that
the AICVic retained a legal practitioner to provide ongoing assistance to members and also to carry out any legal work that may
be necessary to assist members to comply with the *Practice Act.
Michael Benjamin & Associates* had been retained since 1 July 1996
to perform this role. Ms Barrow also commented that if the Court
granted the injunction to the LIV –

*'I would expect that the existence or continuation of non-lawyer
conveyancing in Victoria would be so limited in scope as to pro-
foundly and adversely affect the conveyancing services available
to the Victorian public.'*

Garde continued, saying that a permanent injunction against
the Defendants would not only affect Ms Maric, but every conveyancer in the State by prohibiting them from what they perceive
as their legal right to prepare S.32 statements. He explained that
the Institute had a standing arrangement with *Michael Benjamin
& Associates* in terms of how it conducted its affairs, how it sought
advice, and the documentation which had been drafted and

approved by the AICVic's solicitor. Such S.32 statement did not include the representations and warranties, but in any case the document was not legal work.

Garde also referred to the Second Reading Speech of the previous Attorney-General, Jan Wade, when she introduced the *Legal Practice Bill* which she referred to as the *most far-reaching reform of the structure and regulation of the legal profession for over a century – removing unnecessary restrictions on competition* – so this legislation was pro-competition. The monopoly on the preparation of S.32 statements to solicitors runs contrary to this legislation.

Garde asked the Court to discharge the interlocutory injunction that had previously been granted, with costs to the Defendants. He pointed out that this was a test case in terms of the State of the law.

Mark Dreyfus then addressed the Court and admitted that a conveyancer can arrange all tasks associated with the carrying out of a conveyance, but not the filling out and preparation of a S.32 statement, which quintessentially is 'engaging in legal practice'. However, Judge Osborn observed that *if a conveyancer can't produce any document relating to a conveyancing transaction – they can't do anything.*

Dreyfus went on to say that what the Defendant had done involved the giving of legal advice and that the preparation of a S.32 statement was so complex that only legal practitioners could do them. But Judge Osborn countered that by asking why can't it be that a conveyancer can prepare a S.32 statement in a situation where it does not involve complexity or difficulty?

On that note Judge Osborn reserved his opinion and the two-day trial finished. All involved were exhausted but were galvanised to continue to lobby Government to achieve licensing as soon as possible.

Ironically, the power of the LIV to autonomously apply for an injunction against a conveyancer, was removed a few days later when the *Profession Act* replaced the *Practice Act* on 12 December 2005. Under the new Act such power could only be delegated by the Legal Services Board.

On 19 December 2005, AICVic representatives were invited to meet the Minister for Consumer Affairs and Small Business, Marsha Thompson, and were advised that the Government intended to release the Allen report early in 2006 which would set out the Government's intentions for the conveyancing industry. The Court case was discussed along with the implications if the Court granted a permanent injunction, not only against Ms Maric, but potentially for other conveyancers. Ms Thompson did not specify what the Government's intentions were but AICVic was assured that the Government wanted conveyancers to continue operating their businesses.

CHAPTER 10

LEGISLATION PASSED AND SUPREME COURT'S DECISION HANDED DOWN

THE BRACKS LABOR Government finally released its response to the Allen Consulting Group's report on Conveyancing in January 2006. It stated that the most significant restriction on conveyancing in Victoria was the requirement that only legal practitioners registered under the *Profession Act* could undertake 'legal work' associated with a conveyancing transaction. It also acknowledged that the biggest issue facing conveyancing regulation was the need for adequate consumer protections –

> *'Given that the sale and purchase of a house is the largest transaction that most people will make, it is important to ensure that consumers can be sure that they will not suffer loss from activities that are beyond their control.'*[1]

The Government also acknowledged the need to promote competition within the marketplace and to harmonise legislation with other jurisdictions. It referred to the 2004 report of

---

1 Victorian Government's response to Allen Report – 19 January 2006.

the NCC which found that Victoria's retention of restrictions on conveyancers undertaking 'legal work' –

- reduced the potential benefits to consumers and
- was not consistent with practices in most other jurisdictions.

The NCC report went on to say –

'Because Victoria currently has a restriction on conveyancers doing legal work, for which no net public benefit had been established, the NCC holds that Victoria has not complied with… its obligations under the National Competition Policy Agreement.'

The Allen report set out four recommendations, ranging from light regulation to a full licensing regime. Ultimately the Government preferred Recommendation 3 which was more closely comparable to the regulatory regime for lawyers and real estate agents and would provide greater protection to consumers. This regulatory regime had the following elements –

1. Registration with Business Licensing Authority (BLA) which was part of CAV.
2. Performance monitoring by CAV with disciplinary action for failure to conform to specified performance standards.
3. Providers of conveyancing services would have to hold professional indemnity insurance.

The advantages of this option were that it would address the concerns about minimum education standards, strengthening confidence in the industry, and would harmonise closely with other jurisdictions.

The Allen report also revealed data disclosing that 94% of conveyancers already held professional indemnity insurance (on average to a value of $1 million), so the requirement would be unlikely to be onerous for conveyancers. It also recognised that conveyancers would be required to hold professional indemnity insurance under the proposed Electronic Conveyancing regime and acknowledged that the lack of mandatory cover could impede the Project's progress.

The Government also believed that conveyancers should be able to handle client monies in the same manner as required for legal practitioners and estate agents, which included strict requirements to protect consumers against defalcation. Interest on trust funds held by estate agents was paid into the Victoria Property Fund (VPF) and used to pay compensation for any defalcations that occurred. Legal practitioners were required to pay into the Legal Practitioners Fidelity Fund. The VPF was therefore considered an appropriate fund to hold the interest earned on the monies held in conveyancers' trust accounts.

With respect to qualifications for a person wishing to apply for a conveyancer's licence, the Government deemed that a tertiary qualification and practical experience would be essential and invited suggestions from interested parties about the appropriate courses to ensure conveyancers were skilled. When it came to practical experience the Government proposed that, to qualify, conveyancers only had to complete 12 months' conveyancing experience, under the supervision of a suitably experienced person. AICVic considered that such a short time would be fundamentally inadequate and, as it had recommended in previous submissions, called for a minimum of two years.

The Government acknowledged that some conveyancers who were currently running businesses may not have the required tertiary qualifications but had gained considerable experience within the industry. Therefore, it proposed to grandfather those conveyancers who could, at the commencement of the licensing scheme, demonstrate to the BLA that they had at least 12 months' full-time (or equivalent part-time) practical experience in the industry. Such conveyancers would receive a provisional licence and only gain a full licence once they had completed a prescribed course or, alternatively, had successfully passed an exam to test their conveyancing skills. Provisional licensees could only hold such licences for a period of five years, after which that licence would be cancelled.

In his response to the Allen Report, the Attorney-General, Rob Hulls, drew attention to two main issues that the proposed conveyancers' Bill addressed. The first was that the current regime, i.e. the *Legal Profession Act 2004* (Vic) was contrary to NCP because it allowed legal practitioners to maintain a monopoly on the legal work associated with property transactions. Secondly, the recent collapse of Grove Conveyancing Services highlighted the serious deficiencies in consumer protections under the *Profession Act* in relation to non-lawyer conveyancers, particularly in relation to the handling of clients' monies. He added *While research indicates errors and fraud in the provision of conveyancing services are relatively infrequent in Victoria, when these problems do occur, the consequences are severe.* He confirmed that the Government supported increasing competition in the conveyancing industry.

There was a certain amount of relief within the profession upon reading the announcement of the Government's preference for a full licensing regime. However, there was considerable work to be done before a Bill would be presented to Parliament.

Chris Merritt called AICVic to offer his congratulations on the announcement and commented that in the light of Victoria falling into line with other jurisdictions, it was now only Queensland that was the 'odd man out'.

During this time NSW was in the middle of amending its conveyancing legislation. Whereas in the old *Conveyancers Licensing Act 1995* (NSW) conveyancers were not able to handle a mortgage of more than $7 million, the new *Conveyancers Licensing Act 2004*

(NSW) would remove that restriction. In discussions with Alan West, the Chief Executive Office of AICNSW, who was well experienced in negotiating legislation with Government, he commented how difficult it was to change rules that were enshrined in an Act. It was easier to make changes through regulation, and he encouraged us to follow that path.

Over the next 18 months intense negotiations took place with the DOJ on the contents of the Bill. There were a number of proposals put forward by Government which AICVic pushed back against. For example, at the first meeting with CAV and the Attorney-General's office, AICVic representatives were advised that the LIV wanted licensed conveyancers restricted to only undertaking residential work. Naturally AICVic argued against that proposal, citing other licensed States where there had been no problems with licensed conveyancers undertaking commercial transactions and business conveyancing. However, AICVic did not intend to play hard ball and delay progress and conceded that those who wished to undertake business conveyancing should be required to complete a bridging course.

More importantly, AICVic was adamant that the same definition of 'legal work' that appeared in the NSW *Conveyancers Licensing Act 2004* should be included in the Victorian legislation and would accept nothing less.

With regard to experience, AICVic provided details of the conveyancing course and legal practice course already being taught by RMIT and other registered training organisations which it believed were acceptable courses for licensees.

The practical experience component, however, was problematic. In earlier submissions AICVic had argued for a minimum of five years' conveyancing experience but, in time, realised that there would be little chance of the Government agreeing, because other jurisdictions had a minimum of two years. The Government was urged to change its mind and agree to two years' experience, as one year was patently inadequate.

A Regulatory Impact Statement (RIS) would be required to be undertaken before the Bill could be drawn up and presented to Parliament. CAV conceded it would be a tight timeframe but anticipated having the Bill ready for the Spring session of 2006.

During 2006 AICVic continued to meet regularly with Land Victoria on the EC Project and, in particular, discussed the minimum level required for professional indemnity cover which would be acceptable for subscribers to the EC Project. $1.5 million was mentioned and, although some considered it to be a high-cost burden, it was pointed out that with the introduction of a licensing scheme and a Master Policy, it was possible to get $1.5 million cover for the same premium as was currently being paid for $1 million cover.

Meanwhile in relation to the Maric trial, on 15 May AICVic and its legal team attended Court for a mention by Judge Osborn. He questioned the LIV's ability to continue the action in light of the transition from the *Practice Act* to the *Profession Act*, which did not include an automatic regulatory role for the LIV. LIV however, said that it had had the power delegated to it by the LSB on 3 January 2006. The Judge gave the LIV 14 days to provide him with a copy of the delegation. A few days later confirmation of that delegation was provided by Victoria Marles, the Legal Services Commissioner.

The LSB's actions in delegating power to the LIV angered AICVic, especially in light of the action taken against its member and the ongoing Court case. AICVic representatives immediately arranged a meeting with Colin Neave, Chairperson of the LSB. However, he believed that the delegation of power to the LIV was necessary for the sake of continuity during the transition from the *Practice Act* to the *Profession Act*. AICVic expressed disappointment at the decision and he undertook to raise the matter with the Board. Chris Merritt's article in The Australian on 15 June highlighted the fact that the Board had delegated the power to the LIV and when Chris subsequently contacted the President of the LIV, questioning this delegation, she denied it was targetting conveyancers, stating it was only protecting the public against charlatans.[1] AICVic believed that conveyancers should only be investigated by an independent body, such as CAV, especially given the delicate situation with the unresolved Court case.

At a meeting on 4 July with CAV AICVic was presented with a draft Bill which was to be read in confidence, as Cabinet had yet to approve the legislation. It was encouraging reading, as the Bill included much of what they'd fought for, in particular the ability to undertake legal work.

The positives were –

- A full licensing system administered by Business Licensing Authority.[2]
- The definition of 'conveyancing work' mirrored the definition contained in the NSW Conveyancers Licensing Act 2004, i.e. –

> 'conveyancing work is legal work carried out in connection with any transaction that creates, varies, transfers, conveys or extinguishes a legal or equitable interest in any real or personal property.'

---

1 Article in The Australian by Chris Merritt – 15 June 2006.

2 The final report of Allen Consulting Group had actually recommended replacement of the existing regulatory environment with a minimalist or 'negative licensing' scheme under which a person may provide conveyancing services without a formal licence, subject to withdrawal of the right to practice if they subsequently failed to meet minimum professional standards. Thankfully the Government saw the disadvantages in such an approach, as it would fail to provide adequate consumer protections and would be inconsistent with other Australian jurisdictions.

Conveyancing work was also defined as including –

> 'legal work involved in preparing any document required to give effect to a conveyancing transaction; legal work in the form of advice, or the preparation, perusal, exchange or registration of documents that are consequential or ancillary to such a transaction; and any other legal work prescribed by the regulations.'

- A Master Policy of professional indemnity insurance with cover of $1.5 million to be established.
- Fidelity cover to be established through the Victoria Property Fund.
- An education qualification to be required as well as an experience component.
- A grandfathering arrangement for those who had at least 12 months' experience but had not completed an educational course. The regulations proposed to be made under the Bill would prescribe qualification requirements based on the National Financial Services Training Package which the national AIC had, over many years, assisted in developing with Governments.
- A set of professional conduct rules to be drawn up to deal with such things as conflict of interest, CPD, etc.
- Regulating the handling of clients' monies.
- Inevitably, there were some negatives.
- The educational component was not a specific course but a set of six nationally accredited competencies.
- The experience component was a minimum of 12 months' full time or two years' part-time working under the supervision of a licensed conveyancer or a lawyer.
- Prohibition on conveyancers undertaking business conveyancing – this restriction would be reviewed two years after the introduction of the Conveyancers Act.

- No mandatory CPD (although there was an ability in the Act for the Director of CAV to introduce CPD).[1]
- A licence fee three times higher than that charged for a real estate licence.

The Bill was introduced into the Victorian Parliament on 10 August 2006 and Rob Hulls in his Second Reading Speech, said that the Bill gave effect to the principles adopted in the Government's response to the Allen report and ensured that consumers would be able to enter into one of the most significant transactions of their lives with confidence. He outlined the various points of the Bill and then commended the Bill to the House.[2]

In Chris Merritt's article[3] in *The Australian* on 11 August 2006, he quoted an AICVic spokesperson as saying that the *Law Institute test case had caused major damage to the business of conveyancer, Ms Maric.* His article went on to say –

> *'Now that the Government has introduced legislation opening up the market, the Law Institute should abandon its legal action and pay compensation....For almost a year, Ms Maric's business has been restricted by a Law Institute injunction that has required her to pay solicitors to complete forms that she considered part of her normal work. While the Supreme Court of Victoria has still not handed down its judgment on the Law Institute's test case, Ms Maric's legal bill from that Court action is believed to be about $150,000. In order to comply with the LIV's injunction Ms Maric has also had to pay solicitors to fill out extra forms. That is estimated to have cost her another $80,000. Her business*

---

1   It is disappointing to see that at the time of publication of this book, CPD has still not been made compulsory for conveyancers in Victoria.
2   Second Reading Speech – Rob Hulls – 7 August 2006.
3   Article in The Australian by Chris Merritt – 11 August 2006.

has also suffered a downturn in demand due to notoriety stem-
ming from the legal action. An AICVic spokesperson was again
quoted as saying The Law Institute has a prime opportunity to
make right a wrong that should never have occurred.'

With the Bill finally in the Parliament, AICVic representatives
met with the Shadow Attorney-General, Andrew Mackintosh,
and the Shadow Minister for Consumer Affairs, Wendy Lovell, to
discuss the Bill and the Opposition's attitude. The representatives
outlined their concerns with some elements of the Bill, but were
advised to take a pragmatic view and that unless they were essential issues, we should not insist on any changes, as the Government
could agree to consider our suggestions and withdraw the Bill
with no way of knowing when it would be re-introduced. It was
agreed that it was best to have the Bill passed as soon as possible,
especially in light of the Court case still not being resolved.

Debate took place on the Conveyancers Bill on 12 September
and it passed the Lower House with no amendments. The Bill
then went to the Upper House for the October sitting.

On 25 September, an oral hearing before Judge Osborn was
held. He was aware of the passage of the Bill in Parliament and
had requested that the Government provide him with a timetable
for the introduction of licensing. He canvassed granting a limited
injunction to the LIV restricting the Defendant to only preparing
AICVic template S.32 statements, with the suggestion that when
the Act began, and she had obtained a licence, she would have to
go back to the Court to have the injunction lifted. (In light of the
time that it eventually took for the licensing scheme to start – i.e.
1 July 2008 – this would have been a most unsatisfactory outcome). Greg Garde argued strongly against such a step.

The Judge castigated the LIV and its Barristers for being 'der-
elict' in their duty in not advising the Court that the *Practice Act*

had been replaced by the *Profession Act*.[1] AICVic saw this as a last ditch effort by the LIV to win the argument before it lost its automatic right to bring such action under the *Profession Act* (which became law on 12 December 2005, i.e. 11 days after the completion of the case.)

The entire conveyancing industry was on tenterhooks as it awaited the Judge's decision, as well as the passage of the Bill through the Parliament.

On 3 October 2006 Judge Osborn handed down his decision, finding for the Defendants and dismissing the LIV's application. In setting out the reasons for his decision he said –

> *'In this matter I have come to the conclusion that although the preparation of a S.32 statement may involve the giving of legal advice, I am not persuaded that it will always do so. Accordingly, the fundamental premise of the plaintiff's argument that the defendants will in future engage in legal practice, fails. Further I am not satisfied that the risk that the defendants may engage in the giving of legal advice incidentally to the preparation of a S.32 is such as to justify the relief sought. Accordingly, the plaintiff's application fails and must be dismissed ...Insofar as the law gives rise to any continuing uncertainty in the situation as I have analysed it, this is a question for Parliament to address as it sees fit.'*

---

1   See Court transcript of 25 September 2006 and article by Chris Merritt in The Australian on 29 September 2006. In a footnote on page 2 of his Judgment, His Honour said – *'The Institute did not alert the Court to this legislative change following the initial hearing in this matter. As a result both the exchange of written submissions by the parties and the further hearing of the case were substantially delayed .... The failure to alert the Court of the changes to the legislation was unfortunate given the history of the dispute attending the effect of the implementation of the Practice Act ... and the entirely foreseeable dispute as to the effect of the Profession Act.'*

The question of costs was reserved and at a later hearing Ms Maric was awarded costs and damages.

Coincidentally, on the same day the Conveyancers Bill passed the Upper House of the Victorian Parliament.

The relief was strongly felt and word spread quickly throughout the conveyancing industry. Concern remained regarding the fact that the LIV could appeal the decision and had 28 days to do so. The question was – did the LPB have to approve a decision to appeal?

Many thought the chance of the LIV appealing the decision was less likely, now that a full licensing system for conveyancers was about to be introduced in Victoria. However, on 16 October LIV, advised that it was lodging an Appeal. The industry felt deflated and angry that, despite the Bill becoming law, the LIV continued its action. In addition, AICVic would now have to fund an Appeal.

Many members of the legal profession at CAV and Land Registry were sympathetic to the conveyancers and wanted the LIV to drop the Appeal and accept the Judge's opinion, but the minds of the decision makers at LIV were not to be changed.

As AICVic grappled with the implications of an Appeal, it continued to put pressure on CAV to begin the implementation of the *Conveyancers Act 2006,* so that the whole issue of convey-ancers undertaking legal work could be resolved. In addition, Land Registry was keen for the Act to come into force so that a Master Policy of professional indemnity insurance could be established and licensees could participate in the EC Project. The Government had spent millions of dollars building the system and, if conveyancers could not participate, take-up would be low, which would jeopardise the system's future, as conveyancers were the main stakeholders.

Whilst AICVic was pushing CAV to enable an early start date for the Act, the reality was that it could be as late as 1 July 2008 before licensing began.

The Committee and Management of AICVic had to not only keep pressure on the Victorian Government with regard to the introduction of the Act, but also to deal with the frustration and uncertainty of the Court case and now a forthcoming Appeal. Members of the Committee were committing many volunteer hours while still running their own businesses, which stretched their time between both roles. In addition, although AICVic still only operated with minimal resource, there was still a long way to go, but they were determined.

CHAPTER 11

NEGOTIATING THE REGULATIONS AND THE APPEAL COURT HEARING

WHILST WAITING FOR the Appeal to be heard, negotiations continued with CAV regarding the Regulations to be enacted and, in particular what the Master Policy of professional indemnity insurance would look like. At the outset AICVic reinforced the fact that other jurisdictions ran Master Policies for licensees and that this was the best option. Unless a Master Policy was in place with all conveyancers included, then run-off would not be feasible. A Master Policy was essential to provide consumer protection and establish trust in the profession.

Regarding the practical requirements, CAV was adamant that the twelve months' conveyancing experience requirement was set in concrete. The Government was keen to get as many conveyancers fully licensed as soon as possible, especially to ensure that they could fully participate in the EC Project. Treasury did not wish to raise the bar too high but, in the AICVic's opinion, the bar was set far too low.

The educational qualification to be stipulated in the Regulations was discussed and AICVic again recommended a comprehensive course consisting not only of property law, but also subjects covering running a small business, given potential licensees were aiming to open their own conveyancing businesses. However, CAV reaffirmed that the six accredited competencies set out in the Commonwealth Government national standards, were sufficient and this had to be accepted for the time being. At least CAV accepted the Diploma of Financial Services (Conveyancing) and the Advanced Diploma of Legal Practice qualifications which were already being taught at RMIT and other registered training authorities.[1]

Discussion also took place on the test which was to be taken by those conveyancers who had no educational qualification to satisfy that component for a full licence. CAV nominated VETASSESS, a skills assessment provider experienced in assessing the qualifications and competence of potential workers in many occupations, to design a test and undertake the assessments. Later in the year a focus group meeting was held with VETASSESS attended by representatives from RMIT, CAV and AICVic to discuss what the examination would consist of for those conveyancers wishing to sit a test.

As the Appeal hearing approached, AICVic learned that Mark Dreyfus was not available to represent the LIV, as he was standing for the Federal seat of Isaacs for the Labor Party in the election to be held later in the year.

On 19 April, there was a preliminary hearing before the Master assisting the Appeal Judges, where, despite the recommendation of the Master, the LIV was opposed to any mediation. The LIV requested the Appeal hearing be expedited but the Master did not agree. The LIV began to understand the ramifications of the *Conveyancers Act 2006* (Vic) and the possibility that, if Ms Maric was soon to be licensed, she could not be restrained by the LIV

---

1 A few years later there was a review of the educational requirements for a licence and eventually a higher standard was introduced and an Advanced Diploma of Conveyancing became the prerequisite for a licence.

and could undertake the necessary legal work and give legal advice related to a conveyancing transaction with impunity.

In July, CAV again appointed the Allen Consulting Group to handle consultation on the Regulations under the *Conveyancers Act 2006* (Vic) and had also negotiated an arrangement with VETASSESS to carry out the assessment of those conveyancers without an educational qualification. VETASSESS anticipated having the program completed in a few months ready for testing.

AICVic and the conveyancing profession generally were frustrated, not only with the lack of resolution of the Maric case, but the time being taken to implement the Act. CAV advised that it would potentially be March 2008 before the Act would begin. This was a huge disappointment, as AICVic had hoped that licences would have started to issue by the time the Appeal was heard. Supporters believed that any Appeal Judges would look at the forthcoming legislation and dismiss the case, but AICVic was less confident, as its hopes had been thwarted before.

3 October 2007 was the one-year anniversary of the decision in the original trial and one year since the *Conveyancers Act 2006* (Vic) had passed the Parliament, but AICVic was still negotiating the rules with CAV and also waiting on the Appeal hearing.

An article in the LIJ in October showed the LIV remained steadfast in their view. The President said that the LIV embraced competition[1] – yet it continued with the Appeal and also had refused mediation. The Chief Executive Officer of the LIV, Michael Brett-Young, also called for a delay in the implementation of the EC Project until the insurance concerns of the Legal Practitioners Liability Committee (LPLC) had been resolved and the licensing and insurance for conveyancers had been implemented.

---

1 Law Institute Journal article – October 2007.

During 2007 and 2008 ECV had been building a second pilot system and Gayle Nancarrow of *GLN Conveyancing Services* had been working with their IT team on the practical steps involved in undertaking an electronic transaction, including a financial settlement. It was therefore a huge milestone when, on 12 May 2008, the first multi-lateral electronic transaction with a financial settlement took place on line. The purchaser's representative was Ms Nancarrow and the vendor's representative was David Cummins of *Rainbow Conveyancing*, both members of AICVic. The purchaser's lender was *Bendigo Bank* and the vendor had a clear title, i.e. no mortgage. The whole process took less than 30 minutes and was the first transaction of its kind in the world – a significant event.

At the AICVic Annual General Meeting on 19 October members were provided with an update on the current position of the Appeal and on negotiations on Regulations with CAV. In addition, Ms Nancarrow gave a presentation of her involvement with the EC Project and, in particular, her involvement with the pilot for the new system and how it was developing. She urged members to have an open mind, as some were nervous of the effects that EC would have on their businesses.

Appeal Hearing

The Hearing finally took place on 22 November 2007 in the Supreme Court of Appeal before Justices Marilyn Warren, Marcia Neave and Murray Kellam. J.G. Judd had replaced Mark Dreyfus as the LIV's Senior Barrister and Ms Maric's team were the same as for the original trial, except that Peter Fox had replaced Michael Roberts, who was involved in another trial. Ms Maric was now a 'Respondent' and the LIV was the 'Appellant'.

By the time the Appeal was heard, Ms Maric had completed the required educational course through RMIT. This was relevant

because the *Conveyancers Act 2006* (Vic) would come into operation on 1 July 2008. Accordingly, as she had completed a course in
the prescribed areas of competency, and had completed at least 12
months' prescribed experience, it was expected (and not contested
by the Law Institute) that Ms Maric would satisfy both requirements. She had in fact deposed that she intended to apply for a
licence under the Act *as soon as it is possible to do so.*

In essence, the Notice of Appeal raised three key issues –

1. Whether his Honour, Judge Osborn, erred in finding that the
   preparation of a S.32 statement does not necessarily amount to
   'engaging in legal practice'.
2. Whether his Honour erred in finding that the preparation of
   the particular statement did not involve 'engaging in legal practice' and that the first Respondent would not give legal advice
   relating to S.32 statements in the future.
3. Whether his Honour erred in the exercise of his discretion in
   refusing to grant an injunction.

Counsel for the Appellant put forward that under Ss.14-16 of
the *Interpretation of Legislation Act 1984* (Vic), despite the small
gap between the repeal of the *Practice Act* and the introduction of
the *Profession Act*, the LIV's delegation power was protected. They
also argued that S.32 statements were misinterpreted by Judge
Osborn during the original trial and that a person must apply
legal skill and judgment when preparing a S.32 statement and that
such preparation cannot be done without giving 'legal advice' and
therefore the Respondent had engaged in legal practice. Counsel
also submitted that many of the issues required to be considered
when completing a vendor's statement were extremely complex
and that the consequences of non-compliance with S.32 of the
Sale of Land Act 1962 (Vic) could be 'drastic'.

Greg Garde submitted that in order for the Appellant's argument to succeed on these grounds of Appeal, it was required to show that the preparation of a S.32 statement always required provision of advice. He also submitted that a S.32 statement was not a document which created, varied, transferred or extinguished an interest in land within the definition of 'legal advice' within S.326 of the *Legal Practice Act 1996* (Vic).

Garde confirmed that at all times the Respondent had had a solicitor associated with her practice – first Anthony Sammassimo and then Michael Benjamin – and she would refer any difficult queries about such statements to those solicitors. The Appellant's Counsel did concede, however, that once the *Conveyancers Act 2006* (Vic) had been introduced, and the Respondent had obtained a conveyancer's licence, the LIV had no problem with her preparing S.32s, as the education and experience qualifications would provide the public with the protections required.

Justice Kellam raised the point that if the injunction were granted and the Conveyancers Act was introduced, then the injunction would be irrelevant. Justice Neave confirmed that this would be a relevant factor for the Court when determining whether or not to grant the LIV's application. Justice Kellam read out the definition of what a licensee would be able to do under the new Act and remarked that the scope of work was *all encompassing, i.e. virtually everything that a Solicitor can do!* The LIV's Barrister agreed that once the Respondent had obtained a licence, she would be able to act with impunity but insisted that the injunction needed to apply during the interim period and, once the Respondent was licensed, the injunction could expire. Justice Warren was concerned, however, that the granting of an injunction against the Respondent could be regarded as a *black mark* when she applied for a licence. The LIV declined to comment on this issue.

Greg Garde then addressed the Court and argued that on the question of the *Interpretation of Legislation Act 1984* (Vic), under the *Profession Act*, Recognised Professional Associations (RPAs) disappear and therefore the capacity of an RPA under the old Act did not carry through to the new Act. He believed that this was a deliberate decision by the State Government. In fact, the new Act removed the capacity of the LIV to regulate its own members and reserved that right to the LSB. Accordingly, it was the LSB that should have sought the injunction against the Respondent, not the LIV!

He conceded that the LSB had power to delegate and had in fact given some powers of delegation to the LIV, but strictly under the auspices of the LSB which had the sole authority to seek the injunction. He pointed out that although the LIV was relying on S.14(2) of the *Profession Act*, injunctions were not covered by that part of the Act. Neither the LSB nor its predecessor, the Legal Practice Board, had taken the action against the Respondent, i.e. the LIV had never made application on behalf of the LSB.

Justice Neave went to the fundamental issue with the case when she commented that if you removed preparing the S.32 statement from the work a conveyancer did, then there appeared to be very little for them to do. Justice Neave's comments were encouraging, as this was the very reason why AICVic and its members were prepared to fight the case, as a win for the LIV would have decimated many conveyancing businesses.

Greg Garde pointed out that the Government wished to create competition in the legal services market and had therefore introduced the *Conveyancers Act 2006* (Vic). He went on to remind the Justices that the injunction was discretionary. He also advised that the Respondent had recently completed the Diploma of Financial Services (Conveyancing) and had received a High Distinction.

(The Court requested an Affidavit be provided by the next morning confirming the completion of the course and the date of graduation.) Garde also warned that if an injunction was granted, it may affect the Respondent's application for a licence and may also affect her ability to obtain professional indemnity insurance.

The Court Reserved its Judgment.[1]

---

1 Transcript of Appeal Hearing 22 November 2007 – Law Institute of Victoria v Maric & Anor (2008) VSCA46.

CHAPTER 12

APPEALS COURT DECISION AND LEGISLATION BEGINS

ONCE THE APPEAL hearing was over, negotiations resumed with CAV. Over the past few years, AICVic had dealt with a number of officers at CAV, all of whom had been obliging and easy to work with. One such Policy Officer rang AICVic to advise that the DTF had now decided that a Master Policy was the only option and this would be regulated by a Ministerial Order. The Department was also considering a proposal that AICVic may be the appropriate manager of the policy and asked if they were prepared to take on that role? The answer was an emphatic *yes*.

At a meeting of the COAG Skills Recognition group (a working party looking at harmonising occupational skills throughout Australia) on 27 November 2007, the AICVic representative was advised by Dr David Cousins of CAV that he anticipated that the Act would begin on 1 March 2008 and, because the Act had now been passed, Victoria would be included in COAG's matrix detailing the equivalence of occupations in each State. Agreement had been reached that there was mutual recognition between NSW, SA, Victoria and possibly Tasmania but not WA, where the settlement agents were prevented from undertaking legal work. However, by the end of December, CAV had pushed the start date out to 1 July 2008, the default date.

In early January 2008, discussions resumed with CAV and, regrettably, the Government had now backed away from AICVic managing the Master Policy. It had decided that the cover would be $1.5 million, including run-off and defence costs. Through the Victorian Managed Insurance Authority (VMIA), CAV put out a tender to underwriters, thereby excluding brokers. This was clearly designed to keep costs down.

On 5 February, the Regulations were released and promptly published on the AICVic website seeking members' feedback. There were two sets of regulations –

- Conveyancers (Professional Conduct and Trust Account and General) Regulations 2008 – with 20 conduct rules that conveyancers were expected to comply with, including –
  - ✓ Acting honestly, fairly and professionally with all parties in a transaction.
  - ✓ To only undertake work if the licensee was competent to perform the work concerned.
  - ✓ Not accepting instructions to perform or continue to perform work, if doing so would place the licensee's interests in conflict with the client's interests.
  - ✓ A licensee could act for more than one party in a transaction but if they intended to do so, each party was required to consent in writing to the licensee so doing.
  - ✓ A licensee could advise a signatory to a loan or security document on matters that the licensee considered appropriate.

The Trust Account Regulations were based on the same Regulations that existed for solicitors and set out the requirements for setting up and maintaining a Trust Account.
- **Conveyancers (Qualifications, Experience and Fees) Regulations 2008** – set out the prescribed qualifications for a licensee

to complete, i.e. six nationally accredited competencies, OR completion of a recognised law degree commenced before 1 July 2008, OR successful completion of a Diploma of Financial Services (Conveyancing) conducted by the RMIT, if commenced before 1 July 2008 OR successful completion of an Associate Diploma of Business (Legal Practice) or Advanced Diploma of Business (Legal Practice) conducted by a RTO, if commenced before 1 July 2008, together with a Trust Account course.

It also set out the prescribed experience requirements – i.e. 12 months' full time or two years' part time, as well as the rules regarding provisional licences (restricted to five years) – and the fees which were based on fee units, enabling them to be increased annually.

Unsurprisingly, members with no recognised educational qualifications were worried about their futures and the possibility of them obtaining a licence. AICVic Committee members and staff spent time assuring members that, due to the grandfathering arrangements, they had five years in which to obtain a full licence by either undertaking a recognised educational course or by sitting an examination through VETASSESS, which would be a quicker way of qualifying. The VETASSESS examination would not, however, be a soft option.

Appeal Court Decision

On 19 March 2008 the Supreme Court of Appeal handed down its decision and it was unanimous – **Appeal dismissed** – LIV to pay the Respondents' costs of the Appeal.

The relief was palpable. The initial hearing, the trial and the subsequent Appeal had taken a huge toll on all concerned and conveyancers could now look forward to getting back to work without the threat of litigation. The profession also had the Conveyancers Act to look forward to and a brighter future for all.

However, costs and damages now had to be negotiated with the LIV. The Committee accepted Michael Benjamin's advice to employ a 'costing expert' to determine the costs accumulated. Although it could cost as much as $10,000, the expert would go through everything forensically, so AICVic considered it worthwhile.

By late May, AICVic was advised by CAV that the underwriter for the Master Policy would be *Resource Underwriting Pacific*. This was extremely disappointing, as there was no broker involved and AICVic had been left out of the decision making. (Subsequently CAV reverted to the original idea of AICVic co-managing the Policy with a broker.)

By mid June, BLA advised that an interactive online application for a licence would be available on 24 June. If a conveyancer was operating under a proprietary limited company, the company would require a licence as well as at least one Director of that company. An application for a licence must be completed at the same time as an application for professional indemnity insurance under the Master Policy. The initial costs associated with licensing and professional indemnity insurance were a significant impost for conveyancers. The fees both for a company licence and a Director's licence were –

Application fee	$385.90
Licence fee	$930.70
Total	$1,316.60

Therefore, if a conveyancer operated under a company, the cost for two licences totalled $2,633.20 plus the professional indemnity insurance premium which was based on the conveyancer's income and began at around $2,600. AICVic pushed back against these high fees, arguing that a licence fee for a real estate agent was only about $260 p.a., but were advised that the Department had just introduced a *cost recovery rule*, to which real estate agents were not exposed.

The Ministerial Order pursuant to S.41(3) of the *Conveyancers Act 2006* (Vic) was published in the Victorian Government Gazette on 12 June 2008 setting out the minimum conditions of the policy. The insurer appointed by CAV was *Resource Underwriting Pacific Pty. Ltd.*; the limit of indemnity was at least $1.5 million per claim; the excess per claim was no greater than $2,500, or $5,000 where the conveyancer was acting for both parties; run-off cover was for a period of not less than seven years for a licensee who ceased being a licensee and it provided cover for civil liability for each person who was an employee of the conveyancing business.

To ensure members were well informed, and to address their concerns, a meeting was held to take them through the Act and the Regulations and the process of applying for a licence. A representative from VETASSESS attended to assure attendees that their staff were there to help. Michael Benjamin also gave a summary of the Appeal. The feedback received from some of the members who had sat the VETASSESS test was that it was challenging but not too difficult.

At a final meeting with Policy Officers of CAV before the Act became law, AICVic asked if Ms Maric could be issued with the first licence. They agreed to discuss this with BLA to see if this could happen. Unfortunately, the first licensee was generated randomly via computer and was issued to a non-member who was unknown to AICVic. In fact, Ms Maric received Licence No. 14.

CAV spent the next 6-12 months setting up a review of the restriction on conveyancers doing business transactions. The review would also cover CPD which would not be introduced until the second year of licensing. CAV indicated that AICVic would be put forward as the body to administer the scheme.

On 1 July 2008 the Conveyancers Act 2006 (Vic) and Regulations began which allowed for a grandfather period of only 3 months.

Now that the Act had begun, Victorian conveyancers lost no time in applying to BLA for a licence. Those who had the requisite educational qualification and experience applied for a full licence. Those with the experience component but lacking an educational qualification could apply for a provisional licence by 30 September 2008.

Ms Maric was granted a full licence on 13 August 2008, four months after a three-year campaign by the LIV, which almost put her out of business. Under the scheme, licensed conveyancers were no longer subject to legal action or regulation by the LIV, were backed by professional indemnity insurance, a fidelity fund and had government-approved academic and experience qualifications.

In an article in *The Australian* on 22 August 2008, Chris Merritt wrote –

> *'The scheme means fully licensed conveyancers have the same legal rights as those in most States – they can compete on an equal footing with solicitors for the legal work on property transactions. Solicitors now have a monopoly over conveyancing in just two jurisdictions – Queensland and the ACT.'*[1]

When asked for a reaction by Chris Merritt, AICVic responded –

> *'It has been a long time coming and we have all worked very hard in order to get a regulatory system that will bring certainty to the industry and peace of mind to the consumer.'*

---

1 The Australian article by Chris Merritt – 22 August 2008.

It was thanks all round to AICVic members and the many people who had assisted throughout the last few torrid years. A party was held on 10 November to celebrate the win and the introduction of licensing.

CHAPTER 13

REMOVING RESTRICTIONS ON UNDERTAKING BUSINESS TRANSACTIONS

THE FIRST FEW months of licensing were intense as AICVic manoeuvred its way through the process and responded to the many calls from members and non-members about the new regime. There was a slight delay with the issuing of licences because CAV was required to check with the LSB to ensure an applicant was not a 'Disqualified Person'. Unfortunately, LSB's records only dated from 2006, as all previous records had been kept by the LIV. It took some time for LSB to update its records.

It had been expected that CAV would require evidence to prove a conveyancer's work experience in the form of a Statutory Declaration to submit with the licence application, but this was not the case.

There was considerable disparity between the various RTOs and the total teaching hours their courses provided conveyancers. CAV accepted any RTO teaching the Diploma of Financial Services (Conveyancing), even those where the total hours teaching the course were extremely low. In relation to the first competency under the Diploma, RMIT taught it over 120 hours – 70 hours in class and 50 hours research. Other RTOs taught the same competency over 15 hours – online with no face-to-face classes – causing concern that the course was not rigorous enough.

Initially there was also an issue with some conveyancers still operating without a licence. Despite members being well informed about the introduction of the Act and the process for obtaining a licence, many non-members were either unaware, or were ignorant of the legislation. Those conveyancers who had been slow in making application were shocked after 1 October 2008 when they discovered that the grandfather period of three months had elapsed and they had to comply with new guidelines to obtain a licence. At this point, CAV had still not set up the Public Register on-line, so a conveyancer was unable to check the status of another conveyancer that they may be dealing with, to confirm that they were licensed. CAV were swamped with applications leading to long delays in the issuing of licences.

(On 3 September, a hearing was held before Justice Osborn in relation to the question of costs in the LIV v Maric case. Since the original injunction was granted, Ms Maric had travelled 120 kms each week to Michael Benjamin's office to have him prepare the S.32 statements. The actual cost of each S.32 statement ranged between $150 and $200 but the LIV did not believe the figure was genuine and pushed back. The Judge was critical in his comments to the LIV for challenging the claims and, at a meeting later in the week between the respective solicitors, their demand to investigate the costs incurred by Ms Maric to employ Michael Benjamin to prepare the S.32 statements, was dropped. Difficult negotiations resumed to reach agreement on the amount of damages that the LIV would pay. Offer and counter-offer were made until, with great reluctance on the AICVIC's part, a final amount was agreed, which was only a fraction of the costs incurred. It was not enough to cover the Barristers' and Solicitors' fees incurred by AICVic. Considering the stress that Ms Maric had experienced during this whole unfortunate experience, it seemed unfair that there was no ability to apply for compensation. However, AICVic had no appetite to fight the LIV any further and end up in court again. Its resources had run out and it was time to move on.)

At the end of 2008, CAV again appointed the *Allen Consulting Group* to undertake a review of the prohibition on conveyancers doing the legal work on business sales. In February 2009, it published its report which highlighted that conveyancers were able to undertake sale of business transactions in NSW, SA, NT and WA. The inconsistency with Victorian conveyancers not being able to carry out this work was at odds with mutual recognition principles and the reforms endorsed by COAG which was seeking to create a more seamless labour market in Australia.

Stakeholders who provided a specific view on the merits or otherwise of the current restriction were –

- Australian Institute of Conveyancers (Victorian Division) – who considered that the restriction should be removed
- Law Institute of Victoria, Real Estate Institute of Victoria and the Legal Practitioners Liability Committee – who considered that the restriction should be retained.

The findings of the review were that –

'on the balance of probabilities, the assessment is that the costs of the restriction outweigh the benefits, and that it should be removed. Those jurisdictions that do not have such a restriction do not appear to have experienced significant problems as a result.'[1]

Now that the Court case was over and the review findings had been published, AICVic focussed its attention on its core role of providing education and training for conveyancers. AICVic's

---

1 Allen review of prohibition on business transactions.

resources were still only sufficient to employ a couple of part-time staff to handle an ever increasing workload. What was needed was an injection of funds to be able to employ an Education Officer to establish a regular newsletter and to provide more training sessions. In addition, AICVic was handling a number of calls from members of the public with queries and complaints which took up a substantial amount of the existing employees' time. Other licensed States were subsidised by their Regulator to provide funding for the employment of staff to ensure that appropriate training was available to conveyancers. For many years the REIV had received regular amounts annually, sometimes as much as $500,000, to provide education to its members. This funding came through the VPF, which was the Fund established to protect consumers from defalcations by estate agents and, now, conveyancers. The interest earned on deposits held in Trust Accounts was paid into the VPF and it had accumulated a substantial amount of money. Under S.76 of the *Estate Agents Act 1980* (Vic), the interest earned on the monies held in the Fund could be applied for defined purposes, including –

- Community education, advice or information services regarding... the sale, purchase, lease or transfer of interests in real estate or business;
- The training of estate agents and agent's representatives

As the interest earned on conveyancers' Trust Accounts was now going into the VPF, it was a logical step to apply for a Grant to enable AICVic to employ more staff to handle training and consumer enquiries.

With the assistance of an external consultant, a comprehensive application was prepared and submitted to CAV in May 2009. However, in October, AICVic was advised that, despite the application being professional and well thought through, the

Government had ear-marked VPF money for other projects and it was over-committed. It was recommended that AICVic wait for the outcome of the review into the removal of the restriction on conveyancers undertaking business transactions and introducing mandatory CPD. AICVic was extremely disappointed, believing that they were eligible for such a Grant and felt discriminated against. They considered going direct to the Minister but ultimately did not wish to make enemies of the Department when pushing for more changes to the Act.

In August AICVic was contacted by Professor Sue Campbell, an academic appointed by CAV to review the educational qualification for conveyancers, which would include consideration of CPD. A meeting took place and relevant information was provided to Prof. Campbell to assist her with her deliberations. (In February 2010 CAV advised that Prof. Sue Campbell's report had been received and would be discussed internally over the next few months. AICVic was never provided with a copy of that report and, despite many more submissions and a further review of the *Conveyancers Act 2006* over the next decade, CPD has not been made compulsory for conveyancers, meaning that unlike many other professions, conveyancers still do not have to complete a certain amount of CPD to maintain their licences.)

In October AICVic representatives were invited by CAV to be part of the Financial Services Training Package Expert Working Group, along with representatives from Victorian and interstate consumer departments and a consultant to review the Diploma of Financial Services (Conveyancing). The group was to review all the core competencies and the underpinning skills behind those competencies with a view to updating the course.

It wasn't until June 2011 that legislation was finally introduced into the Parliament to amend the *Conveyancers Act 2006* (Vic) which would remove the restriction on conveyancers undertaking business transactions and on 1 July that amendment became law.

To be eligible for an 'unrestricted' licence, the licensee would need to have completed specific units of competency (which had been introduced in the 2010 Financial Services Training Package which was now the basis of the conveyancing qualification), or have completed a recognised bridging course. In anticipation of the changes, AICVic approached CAV requesting approval of a bridging course called 'Business Conveyancing Law and Practice in Victoria' which it had devised in conjunction with RMIT. Those conveyancers who successfully completed the course were issued with a Certificate of Attainment which they could then provide to BLA with a request for the restriction on undertaking business transactions be removed from their licence. CAV and BLA approved the course which was taught by an RMIT lecturer over three days in October 2012.

One outstanding item that had not been addressed when the Conveyancers Act had been introduced, was the transfer of deposits. Under S.24 of the *Sale of Land Act 1962* (Vic) when a deposit was paid for a property, it had to go into a Trust Account run by a solicitor, a licensed conveyancer or an estate agent and they held it as 'stakeholder'. This deposit could be transferred from an estate agent to a solicitor. However, an estate agent could not transfer a deposit to a licensed conveyancer. CAV prepared the appropriate amendment to the legislation and, in early 2010, legislation was introduced into the Parliament and in due course the *Conveyancers Act 2006* (Vic) was amended to allow for the transfer of deposits.

Professional Indemnity Insurance Issues

By early 2011 it was becoming clear that the professional indemnity underwriter managing the Master Policy, *Resource Underwriting Pacific*, was struggling with the administration.

From the AICVic's perspective, the closed shop arrangement between CAV and Resource, with no broker involved, meant that AICVic was not privy to the types of claims that were being made against the Policy, and therefore couldn't address areas of concern with suitable risk management training. AICVic had urged CAV to appoint a broker from the beginning, as a broker would have monitored claims and raised any issues with CAV at an early stage to ensure that costs did not blow out, which would place the insurance premium pool in jeopardy.

In June, AICVic representatives were advised at a meeting with CAV that professional indemnity premiums would have to increase substantially, i.e. as high as 42%. Earlier in the year, *Resource* had reported a big spike in claims and advised CAV that premiums would have to increase by 50%. CAV rejected this proposal and instructed VMIA to investigate. VMIA called in *AON Insurance Brokers* (AON) who audited the claims and eventually confirmed that there had been a spike. After lengthy negotiations with CAV, *Resource* agreed to set aside $20,000 from the premium pool to undertake a Risk Management Program.

AICVic expressed its disappointment that warnings to CAV had gone unheaded when negotiating the Regulations a few years prior, resulting in an increase in claims. As the body representing many highly professional conveyancers, it was angry that its members were now disadvantaged by the policies which allowed inexperienced people to obtain a licence and join the Master Policy.

A few days after this meeting, CAV announced a review of the professional indemnity Master Policy.

In early February 2012 at a meeting with CAV, AICVic was given approval to run three Risk Management Seminars in August. *Resource* would fund the administration and AICVic would find an appropriate facilitator and venue. *Resource* was also to supply AICVic with claims history and, because CAV would not agree to the program being compulsory for all conveyancers, AICVic suggested that *Resource* should provide an incentive, which was eventually agreed to; conveyancers who had completed ten hours of CPD in the previous six months would receive a 10% discount off their next insurance premium.

CAV was again considering allowing AICVic to take over the management of the Master Policy and this time a broker would be involved. No-one wished to see the policy poorly managed given it was in everyone's interests to reduce claims.

A discussion paper was published in February 2013 and, amongst other options, it contained the proposal that CAV appoint AICVic to manage the Master Policy in conjunction with a broker. In depth discussions were held with AICNSW and its broker, *Austbrokers SPT*, to understand the intricacies of managing the Master Policy and AICVic was able to put forward some positive arguments in response to the discussion paper. In May AICVic received confirmation that the Government had agreed to AICVIc managing the Master Policy with a broker appointed.

Following a public tender process, an Assessment Panel was appointed consisting of CAV, VMIA, DTF and an industry representative. Four Brokers were interviewed resulting in *Austbrokers Countrywide* (who was affiliated with the NSW broker) being appointed as the broker to co-manage the Master Policy with AICVic. *Austbrokers* lost no time in auditing the Scheme to ascertain the best way forward, appointing *Vero* as the Underwriter and made arrangements to take over from *Resource*.

Over time, the arrangement between AICVic, *Austbrokers* and CAV proved to be a positive one for the profession and CAV. *Austbrokers* quickly engaged with BLA to ensure a smooth transition and established a good working relationship.

Each year *Austbrokers* negotiates with *Vero* to ensure that conveyancers are not faced with unreasonably high premium increases.

They negotiated a continuing Risk Management Program with *Vero* in which AICVic provides training to all licensed conveyancers, and for those who complete ten hours of specific training, a 10% rebate in premiums is allowed.

EPILOGUE

THE SMALL GROUP of conveyancers who held that first meeting in 1989 knew their skills and expertise were significant and the value they brought to their legal firms should be recognized. Conveyancers who took the decision to set up their own businesses and were prepared to take the risk of openly challenging the solicitors' monopoly, paved the way for radical much-needed change to their industry.

Organizing themselves into a viable group of like-minded colleagues gave them the strong united voice enabling them to put forward their case to the Victorian Government for the overhaul of outdated laws regarding their profession.

Even when the Government finally agreed to introduce legislation, AICVic had to argue strongly to ensure that the *Conveyancers Act 2006* (Vic) contained the same scope of work definition as existed in the *Conveyancers Licensing Act 1995* (NSW), which, for 20 years, had allowed licensed conveyancers in NSW to undertake the 'legal work' component of a conveyancing transaction. Whilst the Act did include mandatory professional indemnity insurance, fidelity cover and an educational qualification for licensees, the level of conveyancing experience of one year full time or two years' part-time was inadequate, with no mandatory requirement for it to be measured. In addition, a requirement for all licensed conveyancers to complete an agreed amount of relevant CPD annually was not introduced. This remains the situation today and both these deficiencies in the Act impact on claims against the Master Policy of professional indemnity insurance.

Since incorporation in 1991, AICVic has become an important stakeholder representing the conveyancing industry. Committee members and management of AICVic sit on various working parties at State and national level, providing vital input into significant changes to conveyancing law and practice to ensure that the profession's views are heard. Its involvement was vital in the development of the architecture and implementation of the rules for the EC system.

In the early days, it was envisaged that the platform would be jointly owned by the State and Territory Governments but, in time, banks and other investors became the main shareholders. Ultimately the entity became known as Property Exchange Australia (PEXA) which listed on the Australian Stock Exchange in 2021.

The Victorian Government mandated the use of PEXA on 1 October 2018 in order to achieve 100% digital lodgment of conveyancing instruments at Land Registry. One can only speculate how conveyancing businesses would have been impacted if that momentous step had not been taken prior to the COVID-19 pandemic hitting Australia in 2020. Whilst practitioners were restricted to working from home, settlements did not miss a beat and the conveyancing industry can be grateful that it was in such an enviable position.

With the generous assistance of *Stewart Title* as Education Partner, AICVic was able to lease a large training facility and office to continue providing relevant education to conveyancers. With the expansion of its training program, it was fortunate to employ Ann Kinnear as General Manager in 2011. Ann's legal training and business credentials, along with her industry expertise, enabled AICVic to increase membership, produce a weekly newsletter and quarterly magazine, and provide regular educational events.

AICVic has been proactive in providing conveyancers with information on the rise of cyber crime, and the steps required to minimize the risk, which is critical given the extent to which business is now conducted online. Along with *Austbrokers Countrywide*, AICVic negotiated with CAV and the underwriter to include cyber cover in the Master Policy of professional indemnity insurance.

In terms of market share of the conveyancing industry, according to PEXA's statistics (PEXA is currently the sole settlement platform) show conveyancers undertake close to 50% of all transactions in Victoria. It is essential therefore that current and future AICVic members continue to provide a strong voice on behalf of the profession in guiding government decision-making when changes to laws and practices are contemplated.

The Relationship with LIV evolves

For many years after the Court case, there was understandable antipathy between the LIV and the conveyancing profession. Many members of the legal profession, however, had not supported the case and had, in fact, developed good relations with conveyancers. Some lawyers discovered that, whilst losing the monopoly on conveyancing, they were, in fact, gaining work from referrals in other areas of law that conveyancers they worked well with were unable to undertake, such as probate, wills, etc. This was a mutually beneficial arrangement with advantages for both lawyer and conveyancer.

Over time, relations improved between the organisations and there have been a number of instances where the goals and ambitions of the conveyancers aligned with those of the LIV, especially with respect to changes to legislation.

In 2020 the LIV agreed to include an endorsement by the AICVic, including its logo, printed on the front page of the LIV/REIV contract of sale, which was made available to the profession generally. This was a huge acknowledgement and provided consistency and uniformity for the industry.

ACKNOWLEDGEMENTS

THE PATH TO licensing for Victorian conveyancers was long and arduous and would not have been achieved without the dedication and determination of many, both conveyancers and those sympathetic to the cause. The following list is not exhaustive, as there were many people who used what influence they had to convince the Victorian Government of the need for a full licensing system.

The Founding Members of the Victorian Conveyancers Association (VCA) are acknowledged for their bravery in re-establishing the profession of Conveyancers – Trevor Cousley (the first President), Maree Cousley, Ellen Norton, Pauline Barrow, Mary Cocking and Jill Ludwell.

Subsequent Committee Members to acknowledge are the late Charles Dickeson, Gayle Nancarrow, Martin Galea, Sandra Murphy and Helen Mitchell.

Michael Benjamin who became the Retained Solicitor for AICVic members in 1996 and who, to this day, assists them when problems arise. Michael played a significant role in the Law Institute of Victoria v Maric case, assisting Lydia and AICVic throughout that difficult period. George Madden, who worked for Michael, was an invaluable contributor to the positive result.

Lydia Maric, who shouldered the huge burden of a Supreme Court trial. A person with less courage would not have survived such a difficult experience.

The Barristers who represented Lydia – Greg Garde QC (now Mr. Justice Garde KC) and Michael Roberts KC– their knowledge and dedication to the case was all that could be asked of a Defendant's Barristers in such an important test case.

Lawyers Joanne Mackay and Paul Ryan of R.M.I.T., both passionate conveyancing lecturers dedicated to ensuring that the conveyancing course they taught was to the highest standard.

Chris Merritt, Legal Affairs Editor of The Australian (and prior at AFR) who supported the Victorian conveyancers in their fight to gain licensing. His well-researched and passionate articles exposed the injustices experienced by Victorian conveyancers, the lack of a level playing field with other licensed States and, in particular, the unfairness of the Law Institute's case against Lydia Maric.

Many successive Registrars of Title who believed in the conveyancing profession, beginning with Rosalyn Hunt, Barbara Flett, Chris McRae and Ian Ireson.

Officers of CAV who guided AICVic through the intricacies of establishing a licensing system, including Dr Elizabth Lanyon, Murray Bruce and Christine Nigro.

The skilled people at *Austbrokers*, i.e. Brian Salisbury of *Austbrokers STP* in NSW and Tim Considine and Matt Kuc of *Austbrokers Countrywide* in Victoria who assisted AICVic in co-managing the Master Policy of Professional Indemnity insurance after 2005.

Dale Turner, Licensed Conveyancer and former President of the NSW. AIC as well as former National AIC President, and Alan West, former CEO of AICNSW, who were always available to assist AICVic with its travails.

National Council Members who assisted our cause, lobbying governments on behalf of AICVic.

Simon Libbis, lawyer – who provided wise counsel and training for conveyancers over many years.

BIBLIOGRAPHY

The Queensland Solicitors' Conveyancing Reservation: Past and Future Development – Part 1 (2009) – Mark Byrne and Reid Mortensen

The Queensland Solicitors' Conveyancing Reservation: Past and Future Development – Part 2 (2010) – Mark Byrne and Reid Mortensen

Portland Guardian – 15 October 1842

Conveyancers Act 2006 (Vic)

Melbourne Argus – 12 March 1847

Attorneys' Bills and Conveyancing Act 1847 (NSW) 2 Vic 33

Safe as Houses – The History of the Victorian Land Titles Office – Robin Grow

Convict Attorneys' Dismembered Limbs and Certified Conveyancers – Dale Turner (unpublished)

The Application of NSW Laws to Victoria Act 14 Vic No.49

Supreme Court Act 1890

The Torrens System – R.T.J. Stein & M.A. Stone 1991 – Butterworths

Land Rights for Everyone – State Library of South Australia Archive

The Birth of Land Brokers 1987 – Extract from Lawmakers and
    Wayward Whigs – Government and Law in South Australia
    1836-1986 by Alex Castles and Michael Harris
Real Property Act 1862
Legal Profession Practice Act 1915 (Vic)
Legal Profession Practice Act 1958 (Vic)
Legal Practice Act 1996 (Vic)
Legal Profession Act 2004 (Vic)
Committee of Inquiry into Conveyancing – Further and Final
    Report – Daryl Dawson Q.C. (Chairman), David A. Crawford,
    James W. Davies (early 1980s).
Paralegals – Issues in Accreditation – a Paper for the Conference:
    Improving Access to Justice – Jude Wallace, Law Reform
    Commissioner Victoria 19-20 February 1990
Estate Agents Act 1980 (Vic)
Sale of Land Act 1962 (Vic)
Trade Practices Commission Preliminary Report – November
    1992
Trade Practices Commission Final Report – 1994
Case Law – Anthony Hart v NSW Law Society 1989-90
Competition Policy Reform Act (Cth)
Law Institute Journal
The Australian Newspaper
The Australian Financial Review

Milton Keynes UK
Ingram Content Group UK Ltd.
UKHW020443221223
434797UK00001B/1